50 Best
Arena Exercises and Patterns

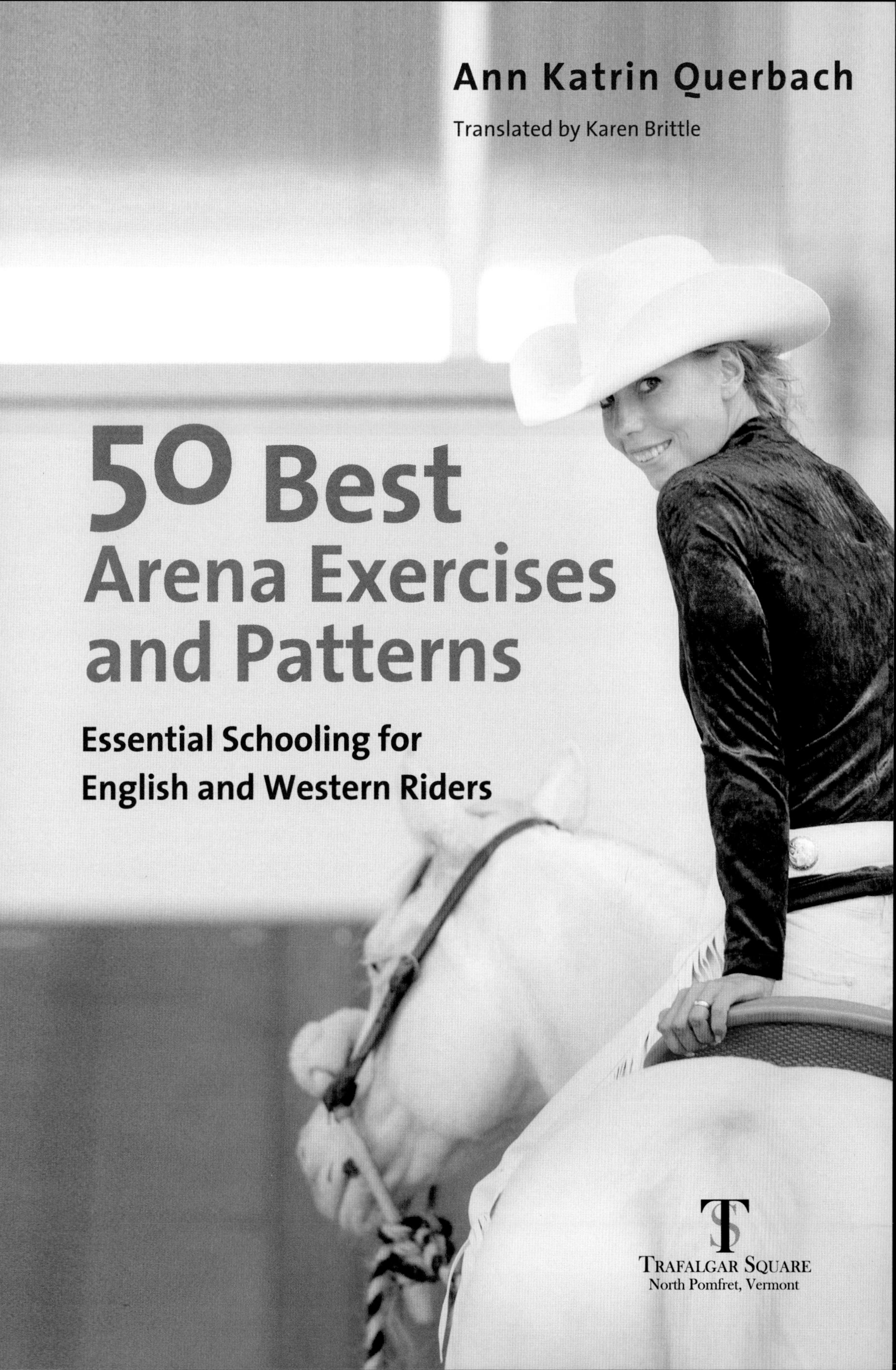

Ann Katrin Querbach

Translated by Karen Brittle

50 Best Arena Exercises and Patterns

Essential Schooling for English and Western Riders

Trafalgar Square
North Pomfret, Vermont

First published in the English language in 2017 by
Trafalgar Square Books
North Pomfret, Vermont 05053

Originally published in the German language as *Pferde gymnastizieren*
by Müller Rüschlikon Verlag, Stuttgart

Disclaimer of Liability
The author and publisher shall have neither liability nor responsibility to any person or entity with respect to any loss or damage caused or alleged to be caused directly or indirectly by the information contained in this book. While the book is as accurate as the author can make it, there may be errors, omissions, and inaccuracies.

Trafalgar Square Books encourages the use of approved safety helmets in all equestrian sports and activities.

ISBN: 978 1 57076 799 9
Library of Congress Control Number: 2016951963

Photographs by Berit Wolf, Franziska Weber, and Jasmin Ziegler
Illustrations by team werk

Design by Kornelia Erlewein
Cover design by RM Didier
Index by Andrea M. Jones (www.jonesliteraryservices.com)
Typeface: TheSans

Printed in China

10 9 8 7 6 5 4 3 2 1

Contents

Introduction 2

1. Finding Your Center—The Correct Seat 4
1.1 Finding Your Center (Evenly Weighted Seat Bones) 6
1.2 Walking on the Horse (Evenly Weighted Seat Bones) 7
1.3 Turn Yourself Around (Correct Turning) 8
1.4 Sensing and Feeling 10
1.5 Relaxed and Following 12
1.6 Deep Breathing 13
Side Note: How Horses Learn 14

2. Learning to Dance 16
2.1 Shifting the Forehand Over 20
2.2 Shifting the Haunches Over 22
2.3 Turn-on-the-Forehand 24
2.4 Turn-on-the-Haunches 26
2.5 Dancing 28

3. Gymnastics and Mobility 30
3.1 Half-Pirouette with Poles 32
3.2 Change Rein across the Diagonal 34
3.3 Simple Serpentines 37
3.4 Counter-Flexion on the Circle 38
3.5 Spiraling In on a Circle 41
3.6 Shoulder-In and Turn-on-the-Forehand 43
3.7 Backing through Slalom 45

4. Rhythm 46
4.1 On a Long Rein (Every Gait) 48
4.2 The Rein-Back (Backing-Up Straight with Poles) 50
4.3 Canter Departure from Volte 53
4.4 Lifting the Back 55
4.5 Counting Canter Strides 57
4.6 Trot-Canter Transitions 59

5. Relaxed and Supple 62
5.1 Precise Transitions 64
5.2 Serpentines 67
5.3 Double Squares 69
5.4 Zigzag Ground Poles 72
5.5 Figure Eight 74

6. Contact and Softness 76
6.1 Cone Game 78
6.2 Trotting Poles 80
6.3 The Diamond (Three Variations) 81
6.4 Leg-Yields with Transitions 83
6.5 Leg-Yield from the Rail and Back 84
6.6 Crossing the Street 85

7. Impulsion or Activating the Hindquarters **88**

7.1 Trotting On from Rein-Back 90

7.2 Extended Trot from Shoulder-In 92

7.3 Extended Trot from Volte 94

7.4 Changing Tempo 96

7.5 Stop Sign 98

8. Straightness **100**

8.1 Counter-Canter 104

8.2 On the Inside Track 105

8.3 Combining Lateral Movements 106

8.4 Bending and Straight Lines 107

8.5 Schooling the Circle with Haunches-Out 109

8.6 Haunches-In on the Half-Circle 110

8.7 Flying Changes 112

9. Collection or Total Willing Cooperation **114**

9.1 Riding Corners 116

9.2 Counter-Volte at the Canter 117

9.3 Half-Circles 118

9.4 Half-Pass at Canter 121

9.5 Cone Game 2 (with Half-Pass) 123

9.6 Shoulder Control 125

9.7 Canter Pirouette 126

10. Special Exercises (Not Only for Western Riders) **128**

10.1 Box 130

10.2 Backing through an L-Shape 133

10.3 Keyhole 134

10.4 Side-Pass 136

10.5 Gate 138

10.6 Bridge 140

11. Special Exercises (Not Only for Jumpers) **142**

11.1 Ground-Pole Pick-Up-Sticks 144

11.2 Ground-Pole Roundabout 146

11.3 Planning the Course—Counting Strides 148

11.4 Gymnastic Row 150

11.5 Follow the Line 152

Thank You 155

Index 157

Introduction

Introduction

The highest goal in riding is establishing the greatest harmony possible between human and horse. When I see horses during daily turnout, they generally move with agility, impulsion, and balance. However, as soon as these same horses are mounted by their riders, it often happens that both horse and rider stiffen up. Both are tense and lack balance.

Celina with her Freiberger mare, Soraya. The goal is the highest possible level of harmony between human and animal.

Because of these observations, I became determined to bring together my experiences working with horse and rider with the goal of establishing unity between them. The result is this book of exercises.

Based on knowledge of classical riding instruction, experience with Western horsemanship and biomechanics, these exercises lend themselves to the development of horses that are motivated at work and maintain soundness over a long period of time.

In this pursuit, it is, in fact, less important what riding discipline you are practicing—the basic concepts are always the same. Optimally, you can utilize the following exercises to realize all of this with your horse: rhythm, a supple connection with a soft mouth, a swinging back, as well as positive muscular engagement over the topline.

I imagine all readers desire a "lively" horse that is sound mentally and physically, and enjoys every training session. Depending on his performance capabilities, we want to develop the horse for diverse equestrian disciplines. To do so, we must refine the aids that support the horse's agility, improve rhythm and suppleness, and develop the correct musculature.

In this book, you'll find valuable exercises, which I have successfully tried with riding students in diverse styles and disciplines. This book is written for riders of both classical and Western riding styles. It simply depends on the rider's knowledge, level, and riding style as to whether she trains only some or every exercise in this book.

All the gymnastic exercises build upon one another, but can also be practiced individually. The first three chapters include exercises that are more basic in nature: How do I find the correct seat? How do I coordinate and feel the forehand and hindquarters of my horse? What easier gymnastic options exist to practice with my horse? In the six chapters that follow, you'll focus in part on the classical Training Scales of the German Equestrian Federation (FN) and Germany's First Western Riding Union (EWU), explaining the most important points of educating your horse. In addition, you'll train these important points with relevant exercises. Each Training Scale is a guideline, which you can use daily to correctly gymnasticize and train your horse, helping him to remain (or become) sound and agile.

The Classical Training Scale consists of the following: Rhythm, Suppleness (with Relaxation and Elasticity), Contact, Impulsion, Straightness, and Collection.

The Western Training Scale includes: Rhythm, Suppleness (with Relaxation and Elasticity), Softness, Activity of the Hindquarters, Straightness, and Total Willing Cooperation. This scale is based on the concept of "ease," meaning the absence of physical and mental resistance, which must be maintained in every stage of training. The idea is to sustain a horse that is completely willing and ready to work. Loss of ease and readiness is most often accompanied by a loss of rhythm, which always means a lack of suppleness will follow.

The overarching goal of each Training Scale, and, therefore, in the education of the horse, is defined in classical riding as a horse that has total willing cooperation and, respectively in Western riding, a horse that has natural self-carriage. In both cases, this means a horse being developed mentally and physically as a comfortable and obedient riding horse. Education is not a drill or training, but rather a systematic "gymnasticizing" of the horse. A horse is willingly cooperative, or respectively has natural self-carriage, when he accepts the aids of the rider with ease and obedience.

Throughout the book I use the term volte, and it applies to both English and Western riders. What is a volte? It is—like a circle—a curved, arena figure, but one that requires a higher degree of lateral bend in the horse because it is a small circle. Voltes are circles of 10, 8, or 6 meters in diameter. Less experienced riders and horses should perform 10-meter voltes when a volte is called for on the pages ahead. Those who are more advanced and who are on horses at an appropriate level of training can use 8- or even 6-meter voltes.

Both of the last chapters in the book bring together special exercises that are (not only!) for just Western riders or just English riders—including trail obstacles and riding over jumps. These, like the gymnasticizing exercises and voltes, are of benefit to every horse-and-rider pair and I encourage you to try them.

Basically, all of the exercises are presented as follows: First, I describe what the exercise does. The next point "What Do I Need?" lists necessary equipment (cones or ground poles, for example). This is followed by "Setting Up," which includes a description of how to lay out the equipment, along with one or more diagrams that make it easier to visualize.

Under the heading "How Does This Exercise Work?" we get to the essence of the exercise, in which I describe its execution, step by step. The next sections "What Is the Horse Learning?" and "What Is the Rider Learning?" are presented in the spirit of reflection, summarizing the lesson and getting to the heart of the takeaway points. Unfortunately, not every exercise will work immediately and without error. Therefore, I have also included the section "What to Do if...." Here, I address the most common mistakes horses make with the exercise (which are often actually the result of common rider errors!). Possible solutions to these common challenges are suggested.

The highest goal in riding is establishing the greatest harmony possible between human and horse. You want to communicate with refined aids and have a willingly cooperative, sound partner (horse) on your side. This is exactly the goal I have set for this book. I hope to convey that every rider can use the exercises to refine communication with her horse and to support every rider in improving her horse's willing cooperation.

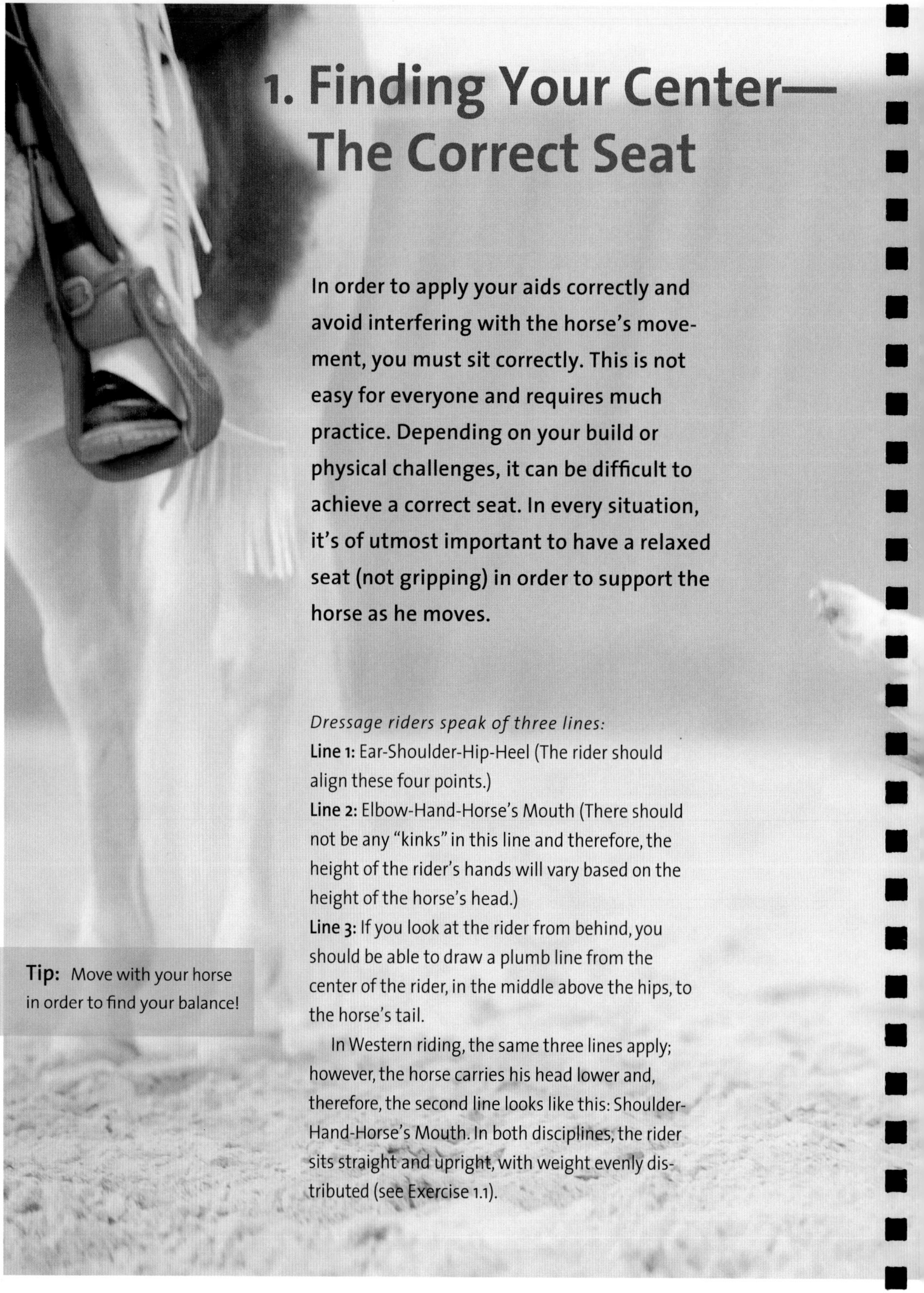

1. Finding Your Center—The Correct Seat

In order to apply your aids correctly and avoid interfering with the horse's movement, you must sit correctly. This is not easy for everyone and requires much practice. Depending on your build or physical challenges, it can be difficult to achieve a correct seat. In every situation, it's of utmost important to have a relaxed seat (not gripping) in order to support the horse as he moves.

Dressage riders speak of three lines:

Line 1: Ear-Shoulder-Hip-Heel (The rider should align these four points.)

Line 2: Elbow-Hand-Horse's Mouth (There should not be any "kinks" in this line and therefore, the height of the rider's hands will vary based on the height of the horse's head.)

Line 3: If you look at the rider from behind, you should be able to draw a plumb line from the center of the rider, in the middle above the hips, to the horse's tail.

In Western riding, the same three lines apply; however, the horse carries his head lower and, therefore, the second line looks like this: Shoulder-Hand-Horse's Mouth. In both disciplines, the rider sits straight and upright, with weight evenly distributed (see Exercise 1.1).

Tip: Move with your horse in order to find your balance!

In order to get a feel for the seat that is centered and straight, you can allow your upper body to swing gently from front to back. After repeating this several times, you will notice that you instinctively find your center.

You can also round and hollow your back, in order to get a feel for a correctly upright upper body. This is important as only then can your spine compensate for the movement of the horse and remain in balance.

The shoulders and hips are level and parallel to one another (in basic position). As you breathe in, pull your shoulders upward; then, move them back in space. As you breathe out, allow your shoulders to slide down your back. The upper arms and elbows lie along the body and the hands are carried out in front.

The upper thigh and knee lie on the saddle, but it's important that no pressure is exerted here. The calf lies on the horse's side. The rider's heel forms the deepest point, but it should neither be forced down nor pulling upward otherwise it is no longer possible for the joints of the feet to absorb movement.

The rider's gaze is forward, as with a well-trained horse, and the establishment of refined communication between horse and rider, the rider's gaze is often all that is required to direct the horse.

The hands do not clench and are carried upright. The thumb should form a small roof on a closed fist. Here, too, the forearm and back of the wrist should form a straight line. With hands that are hidden or turned in, the rein aids are often applied too severely, as the more subtle movement of the wrist joint is no longer possible. Be sure to relax your hands and wrists from time to time before you ride, especially after a long day at the computer.

1.1 Finding Your Center (Evenly Weighted Seat Bones)

In order to apply aids correctly, especially seat aids, it is important to sit evenly and straight in the saddle. In the exercise, you'll practice body awareness as well as correcting the naturally-occurring asymmetry of the rider.

What Do I Need?

Possibly a helper who can handle the horse on a lead or longe line.

Sit on your hands in order to develop a better feel for your seat bones.

How Does This Exercise Work?

(1) Your horse will be led or longed. Take both feet out of your stirrups and let your legs hang.

(2) Now, shut your eyes for a moment and concentrate on the feel of your seat. You must develop a feeling for how both seat bones evenly bear weight. You've succeeded at this exercise when you can always maintain even weight on your seat bones while on straight lines.

What to Do if...?

I can't feel my seat bones.

Sit on your hands, so that the palms of your hands face toward the saddle and the hand's surface is under the seat bones. Doing so enhances the pressure of the seat bones.

I can't manage to maintain even weight on both seat bones.

Here, it's important to first determine whether preexisting physical factors are causing blocks in the hips or legs. Please consult a physical therapist or similar professional.

1.2 Walking on the Horse (Evenly Weighted Seat Bones)

In order to maintain a deep seat in the saddle, it's important to be able to relax the upper thigh muscles and hips. This exercise helps you to sit more deeply and to relax these muscles.

What Do I Need?

A helper to lead or longe your horse.

[a] Here, Evi demonstrates swinging her legs forward from her hips.
[b] Stay seated in the saddle. Evi's leg should not swing quite so far behind her.

How Does This Exercise Work?

(1) Take both feet out of the stirrups. Gently use your hands on the saddle to help stabilize yourself. Now "walk" first with one leg, that is, move your leg forward and backward with a lightly bent knee, as if you yourself are walking on the horse. Do this slowly and pay attention to the stretch. Most of the time, the problem here is that the knee is bent too much, so that the upper thigh and hip can't really mobilize. Make sure your upper body stays straight and doesn't lean to the front or back.

(2) When this exercise works well on both sides, begin to actually walk, meaning that you move one leg toward the front while the other moves toward the back.

If you have correctly executed this exercise, you will now have the feeling that you sit more deeply in the saddle. For most riders, it will now seem like your stirrups are a hole too short, as you are no longer seated "on the saddle" but rather "in the saddle."

What to Do if...?

I can reach my legs forward, but not toward the horse's hindquarters.

First, please get checked out to see if there is a physical problem that is hindering you. Once you've made sure this is not the case, you can begin with stretching exercises on the floor. Stand with your legs wide apart, then bend one knee at a time so that the other leg is being stretched. You should notice a light stretch along your adductors (inner upper thigh muscle). Then, get back on your horse and try again.

I cannot maintain straightness with my upper body.

Most of the time, this is a muscular problem. To do this exercise, you must use your stomach and back muscles. Reduce your "stride" when "walking," so that you no longer have as much stretch in your upper thigh, then little by little increase your stride.

1.3 Turn Yourself Around (Correct Turning)

This exercise lends itself to correct application of the weight aids, so that the horse moves under the rider's weight and can be invited to turn predominately through the seat aids. This exercise will only work correctly when *Exercise 1.1 Finding Your Center* has been completed successfully. By correctly turning the upper body, the inside seat bone will bear more weight. The horse will feel the shift in weight and should move beneath your weight again.

How Does This Exercise Work?

(1) Imagine you have a spotlight in front of your shoulders and another one in the middle of your throat. These spotlights show you the way.
(2) Look in the direction you want to ride, which is the first step to shifting your weight. Now, move your upper body parallel to your horse's shoulders in the direction of the movement. Make sure that your inside shoulder doesn't collapse, which will cause your hips to buckle and your weight to shift to the outside. It's important not to make your turns too wide, or else you'll begin to come out of the saddle and that will cause your relaxed upper thigh to start gripping.
(3) Now ride back and forth in all directions, gaining a better feel for turning. As you do so, try to refrain from using your rein aids as much as you can. It's best to ride on long, loose reins.

What to Do if...?

I can't feel whether my weight is shifting correctly.

> Sit on your hands for a moment in order to check if your weight aids are functioning correctly.

My horse is not turning, although I'm sitting correctly.

> Here it's important to determine if the horse is far enough along in his training so as to really understand weight aids. If this is the case, apply your outside leg lightly on the horse's side, helping to frame your horse. Depending on the sensitivity of your horse, the pressure with your outside leg may be strong or light. As you practice, it's important to always give the lightest aid first and then slowly increase the pressure, so that the horse doesn't have a strong reaction. In order to have a horse that remains sensitive

to the aids, it's important that as soon as he reacts to pressure from your leg, you immediately remove the pressure; thereby, in the end, it should be enough to lay the leg against the horse's side.

I come out of the saddle when I turn.

Let go of the reins and spread your arms wide (as we tell children, play "airplane"). Now turn your upper body slowly from right to left. Make sure that your pelvis stays straight, meaning that it points in the direction that you're turning.

1.4 Sensing and Feeling

This exercise develops your feel for the movement and rhythm of your horse. Here, you'll learn when the horse moves each leg. This is important later in order to recognize exactly when an aid should be applied, influencing the movement of a specific leg of the horse to increase the action or bear more weight, respectively. This is also an important exercise to prepare for trail riding; for example, when you're riding through the woods and a small log lies in front of you. With this exercise, you can prepare to ride your horse safely over such an obstacle.

What Do I Need?

2 poles. A helper on the ground who can monitor whether or not your feel is accurate.

Setting Up: Place a pole at any point on a circle, a few feet off the rail.

With help from Jessy, Mona estimates the distance between foreleg and pole.

How Does This Exercise Work?

(1) First, ride around the outside of the poles at the walk. Concentrate on how your pelvis moves in the saddle. You'll hear this described as a horizontal eight: the pelvis always moves unilaterally slightly upward and forward and slightly downward and backward. When the left side swings forward and upward, the right side swings backward and downward. Ride at the walk until you clearly understand this movement.

(2) When this is the case, concentrate only on one element of the movement, for example, the hip swings forward and to the left. Always when this occurs, the horse is moving his left front leg forward, too. Position a second person on the ground and let them confirm for you whether you can consistently identify when this leg is moving.

(3) Once that works, repeat the same process with the horse's right foreleg. Once you are confident with the forelegs, begin to work at the hind legs. Here, you must have the feeling that your hip bends downward and backward. This means every time your hip moves downward, backward, and to the left, the left hind leg of your horse is moving.

(4) Once you've mastered this on the left side, begin to work on the right.

(5) When you are certain that you can feel each limb of your horse in movement, play a small game with your helper. This person calls out a specific leg of the horse (for example, "Right hind") and you must call out "Now" every time this leg moves forward. The helper then changes to any other leg and you must again call out.

(6) Once you have perfected this, you can take the next step, beginning to ride over the poles on the circle at the walk. Try to identify for your ground person which of the horse's front legs crosses over each pole first. Once you've got that, tell her which hind leg is crossing over each pole first. The goal is to feel when a specific leg of the horse moves over the obstacle.

(7) When you have also mastered this exercise, you can again go one step farther. Before the horse crosses the pole, try to feel the distance at which he has arrived there. Is he too far away and, therefore, has to take an extra-long stride? Is he too close and can only fit in a tiny step? In both cases, you should feel that the rhythm is briefly broken. Or, is the distance correct and you consistently have the right distance to the pole?

(8) Once you have successfully completed this exercise at the walk, you can try at other gaits.

What to Do if...?

I feel the individual legs incorrectly or too late.

Practice makes perfect, so don't give up and do allow a second person to help you. Concentrate on one specific leg. Allow the second person to tell you when this leg is moving and try to feel what your pelvis is doing in this moment. Eventually, you will be able to link your body awareness with the moving leg.

My horse always has an incorrect distance from the poles.

In this case, you should really frame your horse with your leg aids and plan your path ahead. Count how many strides your horse needs to take along the correct path and for the right distance, and hold to this count as you ride between the poles. To do this, you may have to drive your horse forward or take him back a bit. This advice is based on the assumption that there is an even distance between the poles.

1.5 Relaxed and Following

Developing a relaxed following seat while maintaining a centered position is one of the most important cornerstones of riding. The hips are the connection between horse and rider. The rider should not deliberately pump with her seat; rather, she should allow herself to be carried by the horse's movement.

What Do I Need?

A ground person to longe the horse.

How Does This Exercise Work?

(1) The trot is the most difficult gait. Therefore, I'll describe the exercise at this gait, though it can certainly be practiced in any gait you choose. Secure the reins to the saddle horn, surcingle, or handhold. Your ground person should be familiar with both the horse and the longeing and whip aids.

(2) Now trot on the longe line and let your horse move you.

What to Do if...?

After a couple of trot strides, I lose my balance or tense up and can no longer move with the horse.

Bring your horse down to a walk and simply start over again. This time, lift your arms to head level and pretend you are holding a mobile phone with your left hand, meaning you make a fist but stretch out both your little finger and thumb. With your right hand, make a "V for Victory" sign by extending your pointer and middle fingers. The rest of the hand makes a fist.

Now, when your helper tells you to do so, switch the hand signals to the other side. You'll notice that it is really not as easy as it sounds, and is always good for a laugh. This will relax you. Concentrate on your hands and you'll find it much easier to move with the horse.

1.6 Deep Breathing

The goal of every rider is the highest possible level of harmony between human and horse, supported by precise communication. The horse mirrors the human. You can take advantage of this fact when applying your aids and seat. Therefore, the intention of this exercise is to build positive engagement and tone throughout the body. First for the rider: As soon as you can develop positive tone, the horse will mirror you and also complete the desired exercise with the same positive engagement. In order that you don't tense up and forget to breathe, here is a small exercise for daily use. By and by, you will be able to effectively maintain this positive engagement of the body, without tensing up.

What Do I Need?

You may need a second person to lead or longe the horse.

Tip: This exercise can also help a fearful rider to relax.

How Does This Exercise Work?

(1) As you breathe in through your nose, spread your arms wide out to the side. Turn your palms up and bring your hands together above your head. As you slowly exhale out of the mouth, spread your arms wide again. Allow your arms to travel down to your sides, letting them hang, relaxed.

(2) Repeat this exercise. Feel it in your body. When you feel your chest lift as you breathe in and feel it in your belly as you exhale, you have successfully completed the exercise. Ask your helper to observe and determine whether you have also maintained your straight lines of position throughout.

What to Do if...?

I can't hold my arms above my head.

If it's difficult for you to hold your arms above your head, you can begin by crossing your arms behind you as you breathe in. Most of the time, the muscles just need to be loosened up.

I hollow my back or stick my head out in front of my body.

This shows weakness in the back muscles. Try this exercise on the ground first. Stand on the floor with your feet hips' distance apart and complete the exercise as described above.

Side Note: How Horses Learn

This is the essential question of both basic and advanced training.
Let's try an experiment: "Silence is praise enough."

What Do I Need?:
A helper.

(1) Leave the room. Your helper thinks of a task (e.g. when you get back, you should sit down in the chair that's on the left). Reenter the room but your helper should *not* tell you what she wants you to do. The only thing she can do is say, "No." Begin to walk around the room slowly. As soon as you turn in the wrong direction (away from the chair), the helper says "No." Each time you move away from the chair, she says "No." When you finally do sit down on the chair, your helper says nothing. (Remember, she's only allowed to say, "No.")

How do you feel? How long did it take you to figure out what was required?

(2) Now begin with the same exercise as in Step 1 but with a new task. The difference is that instead of saying "No," this time your helper can say "Yes" when you get closer to achieving the task she has chosen. The helper may also use the word "Yes" once you have completed the task successfully.

(3) For the third step, I want to ask you to do the same exercise again. Now, your helper can use the words "Yes" and "No" as if you were playing the "Hot-Cold" game. She can guide you to complete a task such as picking up a framed photo.

How do you feel? How long did the exercise last? What do you notice? Did the exercise clearly go faster this time? Did you feel happier and more motivated? Was the game easier?

What Does This Have to Do with Riding?

Let's say you want the horse to learn a cue, such as bending around the inside leg in a turn.
Step 1: You apply the inside leg and weight.
Step 2: You support the horse by positioning him with the inside rein and by maintaining a regulating (guarding) outside rein and leg.
Step 3: The horse bends for a moment. You reward him immediately and yield the aids you used in Step 2. So, you come to the realization that both horses and people learn most quickly and stay motivated through clear direction and praise.
An exercise is repeated like this until the horse responds immediately to the initial aids. This leads to precise and harmonious communication between human and horse.

2. Learning to Dance

The Aids

A correct aid is always a coming together of all the aids. First off, I'd like to explain the individual aids.

The Weight Aids

- Weight aids *evenly distributed on both sides.* This is used on all straight lines. This means that both seat bones bear weight evenly. *See Exercise 1.1, Finding Your Center.*
- Weight aids applied on *one side*. This is used on all bending lines and lateral movements. Only one seat bone is weighted.
- Weight *off the back*. This is used when riding in a light seat.

The Leg Aids

- When discussing leg aids, we are referring to the rider's calf, which should hang relaxed against the horse's side and support the effort to drive the horse. Only for correction, you can bring in the artificial aids of spur and/or whip. You must distinguish between the following leg aids: (1) a *forward-driving* leg aid, during which the leg is applied "at" the girth (really a hands-width behind the girth) and helps to activate the hindquarters; (2) the *sideways* leg aid, which encourages the horse to cross over with his legs; and (3) the *regulating (or guarding)* leg aid, which is used to provide a boundary on bent lines and during lateral movements, such as the leg-yield.

  The rider's forward-driving leg should always be used to support the horse's hind leg on the same side. To do this requires that you can feel when the horse activates each hind leg.

Positioning of the sideways-driving leg can change for the purpose of making corrections. For example, when the lower leg is applied at least two hand-widths behind the girth, we're moving the hind end of the horse over. Applying the leg aid just slightly behind the girth moves the shoulder of the horse instead (see Exercise 2.1).

Your goal is a horse that can be ridden from the weight and leg aids alone, and that you only need the rein aids to clarify a desired exercise for the horse. So, it makes sense that the weight and then the leg aids should always be applied first, and only after that the rein aids. This sequence happens within milliseconds so that all the aids always support the last aid given. And, this can vary based on training level and riding style.

The Rein Aids

- Whenever a direct rein is used, a yielding rein aid must always follow, such as when the *inside rein* is used to position the horse. A *regulating (or guarding)* rein sets a boundary for the horse on the outside during positioning and bending. An *opening* rein is useful for young horses (or at the beginning of training for a horse at any age), as it effectively "shows the horse the way."
- Your hand position plays an important role. If you carry your hands wide and deep, you support the horse moving forward and downward in a "stretchy" frame. If you carry your hands high and tight, the horse will carry his head higher. As soon as the horse no longer needs an adapted hand position for support, you should resume the straight line: elbow-hand-horse's mouth (dressage) or shoulder-hand-horse's mouth (Western), in order to avoid disturbing the horse. A supple wrist is important. The hands should be held upright and kept closed with the thumbs held relaxed, forming a small roof over the fist.

The Voice

- With young horses that are at the start of training, the voice can be used purposefully as an additional supporting aid.

In order to avoid having your horse become dull to the aids, you should observe the Three-Point Rule (which applies to all the aids!):
(1) First, you should ask your horse carefully, using just the right amount of pressure you want him to respond to.
(2) Second, ask with the same aids, but with stronger pressure.
(3) Last, build the pressure up so that your horse immediately executes the required exercise. As soon as the horse executes the desired exercises, reward him with your voice and a release of the aids.

Your horse will quickly learn that it's to his benefit to respond to the first request and, thereby, stay sensitive to the aids. Don't ever become unfair or emotional in a negative sense. When you strengthen your horse through ample praise, you will motivate him to give you a small gift. You'll notice that the horse thinks about how to please you, and he will want to do the exercise again in order to earn your praise.

Note:
Horses cannot concentrate for a very long time (about 1 to 10 minutes). After he has completed an exercise, reward your horse with praise, walking, halting, and release of the aids.

Half-Halt: The coming together of all the aids in preparation for every transition.

Full Halt: The coming together of all the aids always leading to the halt.

2.1 Shifting the Forehand Over

In this exercise, the horse learns to move his forehand sideways, without crossing his hind legs. You're training flexibility of the forehand and counter-flexion *(see Exercise 3.4)*. With this gymnastic exercise, you can enhance willing cooperation.

What Do I Need?

3–4 cones.

Setting Up

Position the cones on the centerline or down a long side of the riding arena, at a distance about 26 feet (8 m) apart.

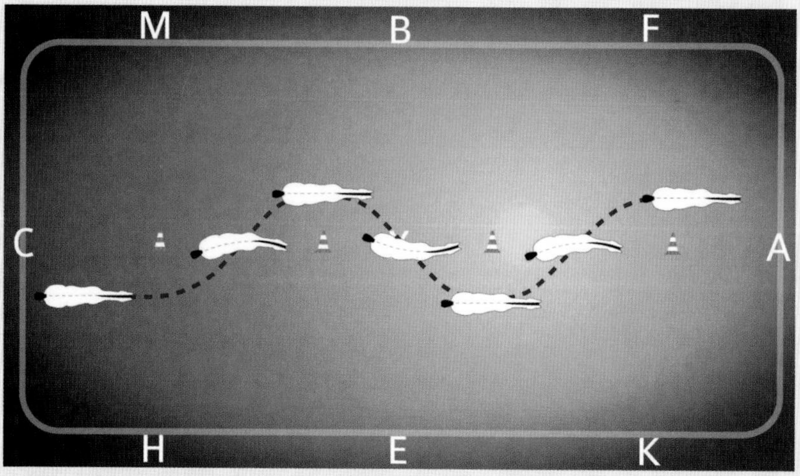

How Does This Exercise Work?

(1) Ride a serpentine at the walk around the cones on the centerline. As you do so, your horse should not turn, but instead just shift his forehand.

Aids: Tracking left, turn onto the centerline at the walk. Ride straight past the first one. When your horse's croup is in line with the first cone, begin to position the horse to the right, using your right rein. Your horse is now in a counter-flexion. The left hand gives, freeing him to move to that side. The right leg presses at the girth, while the left leg guards on the horse's side. Shift your weight to the right. Look in the direction in which you wish to ride (here, to the left). The hindquarters follow, but the legs do not cross. When you reach the next cone, release all your aids and ride straight ahead once more. When the croup of the horse is in line with the second cone, position your horse in the other direction and continue the pattern.

(2) If this exercise works well at the walk, you can try it at the trot.

Heads Up! Make sure that as your horse is moving sideways, he's moving forward, as well.

Evi shifts Nena's forehand toward the outside, while at the same time, Nena is positioned slightly to the inside.

What Is the Horse Learning?

Flexibility and prompt reaction to the rider's aids. Counter-flexion. To lift through the shoulder.

What Is the Rider Learning?

Coordination of hand and leg. Feel for how the horse steps laterally.

What to Do if...?

My horse just walks straight ahead.

Give a stronger leg aid. Clearly give with the outside rein in the desired direction by pointing the way with this rein.

My horse also crosses the hind legs.

Make sure that your leg is not too far back. It should lie just about 1 inch (2–3 cm) behind the girth.

2.2 Shifting the Haunches Over

With this exercise, horse and rider learn the coordination of the forehand and the haunches. The horse will step farther under his center of gravity and lift through the shoulder. Weight will transfer from the forehand to the haunches. This exercise increases the willing cooperation of the horse. Your riding aids will improve.

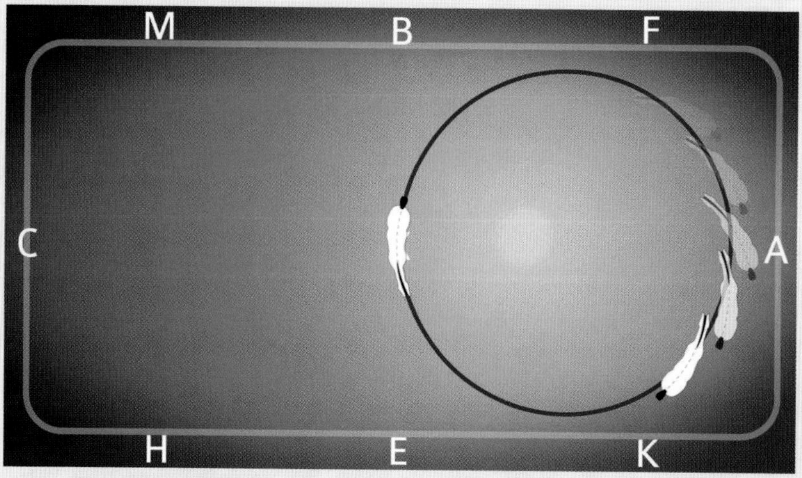

How Does This Exercise Work?

(1) Ride a circle at the walk, 3–4 feet (1–1.3 m) away from the rail. Push your horse's haunches so far to the outside that his inside hind hoof steps into the hoof-print of the outside front hoof.

Aids: Ride a circle tracking left. Using your left rein, position your horse to the inside and use your regulating right rein on the outside. Shift your weight to the left. Drive with your left leg. Look in the direction that you want to ride. Your shoulders stay parallel to your horse's shoulders. To shift his haunches out, bring your left leg back clearly. The right leg lies in a guarding position against the horse's side. Shift your weight to the left and turn your upper body at the same time.

Heads Up! Make sure you do not fold at the hips. Your inside shoulder stays open and your inside leg stays long. The horse stays slightly positioned to the inside. Look along the line of your circle. Turn your hips parallel to the horse's hindquarters.

(2) Now ride this exercise to the right.

(3) Test the success of your training when you resume riding the whole arena. Your horse's stride should now be noticeably more ground-covering.

Nena willingly yields with her active hind leg.

What Is the Horse Learning?

To step deeper under his center of gravity. To shift weight from the forehand to the haunches. To lift through the shoulder. Coordination of the forehand and haunches. To react with sensitivity to the rider's aids. This exercise trains even muscular development, helping to overcome naturally occurring asymmetry. Develops the muscles of the horse's topline.

What Is the Rider Learning?

To coordinate and feel the forehand and hindquarters of the horse. A sense for how the inner hind leg steps underneath the horse. Refinement of the aids.

What to Do if...?

In the course of the exercise, my circle keeps getting smaller.

The horse is leaning too heavily on the forehand. He's not responding sufficiently to your aids. *(Go back to Exercise 2.1.).*

My horse is crossing his forelegs as well.

Be careful not to position your horse too strongly. In this case, your horse is stepping past the center of gravity with his inside hind leg.

Try to solve this problem by executing shoulder-in down the long side of the arena (see ch. 8 for further explanation of lateral movements).

2.3 Turn-on-the-Forehand

The turn-on-the-forehand is a gymnastic exercise that helps your horse loosen up. Through this exercise, the horse will lift himself more through the lumbar region of his spine and, consequently, lengthen his stride. The turn-on-the-forehand is a standard component of a dressage rider's basic education. In this exercise, the horse turns around the inside foreleg. The forehand walks in place, while the hindquarters move in a half-circle around the forehand. The hind legs cross.

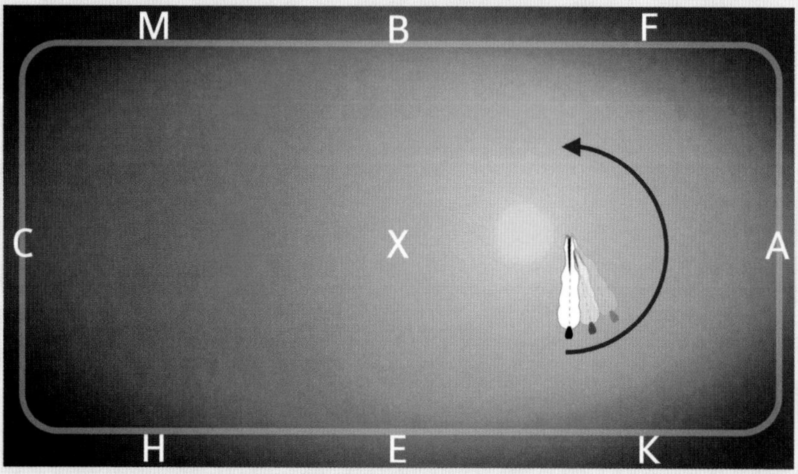

How Does This Exercise Work?

(1) At the walk, ride several feet off the rail, tracking right. Choose a point to halt. The hindquarters should turn 180 degrees around the forehand.

Aids: Shift your weight to the left seat bone. As you do so, apply your left leg far behind the girth. The right leg lies at the girth in a guarding position. The left rein positions the horse to the left. Take a light contact with the right rein, in order to regulate the horse's outside. The hind end should now move 180 degrees counterclockwise.

> **Tip:** Look in the direction you want the horse to turn. Don't look down at the neck. Turn your upper body 90 degrees in the relevant direction. By doing so, you'll automatically distribute your weight correctly.

(2) Now, ride the turn-on-the-forehand tracking left.

Using ground poles, Juliane has set up an optimal boundary for training her horse to do a turn-on-the-forehand.

What Is the Horse Learning?

Sensitivity to the rider's aids. Moving the hindquarters without moving the front end. Crossing the hind legs. Relaxation and suppleness.

What Is the Rider Learning?

Refinement of the aids.

> **Tip:** If you are attempting this exercise with an inexperienced horse, it is important to pause after every step to reward the horse. The horse learns more quickly and stays motivated.

What to Do if...?

My horse walks forward or sideways with his forehand.

In this case, your outside guarding rein is not influencing the horse. Increase the contact on the outside rein.

My horse kicks out at my leg.

Make sure you are not applying your aids too harshly. Apply deliberate pressure with the driving leg and check to be sure your leg is lying correctly. If the problem does not resolve, it is likely a dominance issue. You should resolve this with groundwork.

My horse crosses with his front legs.

Your inside rein is being applied too strongly.

2.4 Turn-on-the-Haunches

The turn-on-the-haunches is an exercise that collects the horse. It is equally useful for dressage riders and Western riders. Dressage riders use it to train the horse to shift more weight onto the hindquarters (and it is a required element in dressage tests). The Western rider can utilize the turn-on-the-haunches as a precursor to training the horse to spin.

In a turn-on-the-haunches the horse turns 180 degrees around his inside hind leg. The front legs cross as they turn around the hindquarters. As this is happening, the hind legs should move in a volte and should not cross. Only in the last step back to the track, should there instead be a forward-and-sideways movement, during which the hind legs may also cross.

What Do I Need?
2 poles.

Setting Up
Make a corner by placing the two poles at a 90-degree angle on the ground.

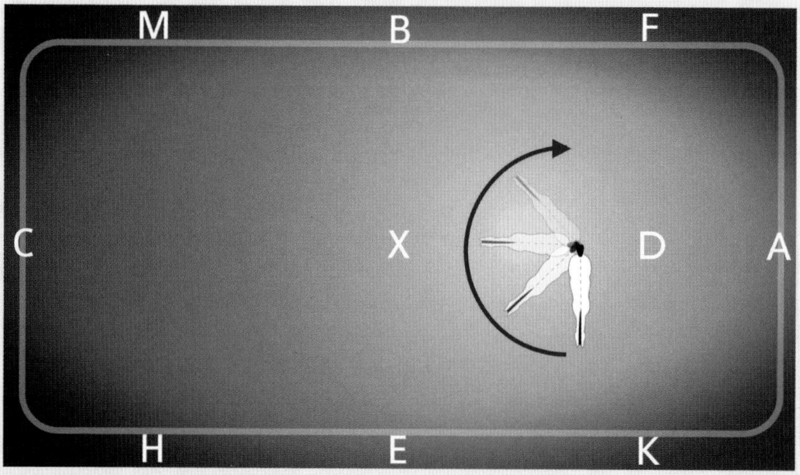

How Does This Exercise Work?

(1) Ride up the centerline. Choose a point and begin to turn there, at the walk. In the beginning, your turn will resemble a volte. As you do the exercise, try to make your volte smaller.
(2) At the walk, ride into the corner you have created with the ground poles and use the poles to guide you as you execute a turn-on-the-haunches.
(3) Now, try a turn-on-the-haunches at the dressage letter D (see diagram). Don't be surprised if you end up somewhat farther from the point, in the direction toward X. That is correct, as your horse is turning around his inside hind.

Aids: For a turn-on-the-haunches to the left: Tracking left, use your left rein to position the horse to the left. There is contact on the right rein, which lies against the horse's neck in order to set an outside boundary. Shift your weight onto the left seat bone. Drive with both legs, preventing the horse from stepping backward. The left leg applies less

Daleo willingly yields as his front leg is driven around.

pressure, as it must allow enough room for the horse to turn. The right leg presses at the girth, thus inviting the lateral movement.

Tip: When turning, bring your right shoulder slightly forward and look to the left. Reverse your aids to execute a turn-on-the-haunches-to-the-right.

What Is the Horse Learning?

Acceptance of the leg and sensitivity to the rider's aids. To shift more weight onto his haunches. To cross with his legs. Collection.

What Is the Rider Learning?

To refine the aids.

What to Do if...?

My horse walks with his hind end also.

Trick your horse a little by executing the turn-on-the-haunches out of a rein-back.

My horse falls on the forehand.

Back your horse into the turn-on-the-haunches and apply a stronger outside leg aid.

My horse is turning around the wrong hind leg.

On the side where your horse is having this problem, you should approach the turn-on-the-haunches from a leg-yield. This way your horse will automatically bear more weight on his inside hind leg and turn himself around that leg.

My horse falls onto his inside shoulder.

Ride at the half-pass in the applicable direction (see ch. 8 for further explanation of lateral movements). In this way, your horse will lift through the shoulder. Immediately following the half-pass, ride the turn-on-the-haunches.

2.5 Dancing

This exercise combines the turn-on-the-forehand and turn-on-the-haunches. This combination increases the horse's agility and attention. Therefore, he can better respond to different positions of the rider's leg, which develops the willing cooperation of the horse. Your horse will become more flexible in his spine (especially in his loin area).

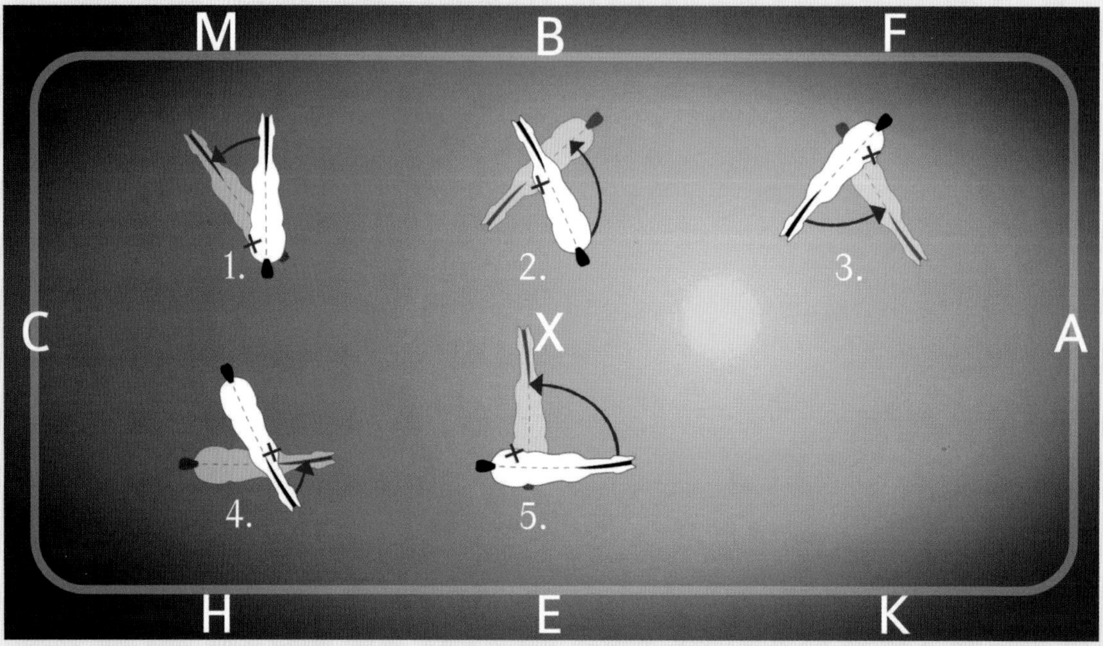

How Does This Exercise Work?

(1) Tracking left, ride 3–4 feet (1–1.3 m) from the track. Choose a random point.

(2) Begin, for example, with two steps of a turn-on-the-haunches to the left (no. 1 in diagram). As you do so, lightly position your horse to the left. Shift your weight to your left seat bone. Use your right leg to drive the horse's forehand to the left.

(3) Pause. Then, for several steps execute a turn-on-the-forehand to the right (no. 2). Using your left rein, position your horse to the left. Shift your weight to your left seat bone. Use your left leg to drive the horse's haunches to the right. Again, pause.

(4) Now, again ride a few steps of turn-on-the-haunches (no. 3) and a few steps of turn-on-the-forehand (no. 4). Conclude the exercise with a few steps of turn-on-the-haunches (no. 5). Pause in between each turn. Observe these pauses so that the horse stays motivated and doesn't become overwhelmed. But, as the exercise progresses, make your pauses shorter.

What Is the Horse Learning?

Sensitivity to the rider's aids (especially the leg aids). Crossing with his legs. Flexibility in positioning.

What Is the Rider Learning?

Refinement of the aids. A feel for the various turns.

Heads Up! Don't use your rein to pull your horse in the desired direction. Guide his turn with your leg.

Tip: Look in the applicable direction. As you do so, turn your head 90 degrees.

What to Do if...?

My horse is losing his balance and straightness at times.

Is the horse overwhelmed, perhaps because the turns are coming too quickly in succession? If not, the rider's inner leg can often be responsible for this problem. Be aware that you do not stretch your inside leg out in front of you or too far away from your horse. Your inside leg should just be a slight distance from the horse's side.

My horse executes his favorite exercise, without my giving him the aids.

In order to avoid having your horse anticipate the exercise, make sure to include forward movement and rein-back in between the turns.

3. Gymnastics and Mobility

The goal is a mentally and physically sound horse that takes pleasure in every training session.

How do you motivate the horse to engage with you actively? Using ground poles and cones as visual aids can help all horses (not only the young ones) stay focused and motivated.

While warming up your horse, riding basic exercises such as Change Rein across the Diagonal (Exercise 3.2) at walk and trot prepares him well for subsequent "gymnasticizing" exercises.

The Simple Serpentine is a very basic ring figure that nonetheless has good gymnastic effects. This exercise loosens and stretches your horse's muscles. Combined with other exercises, this can be used to check your horse's rhythm, suppleness, contact, and straightness. To further condition the muscles, for example, to achieve correct longitudinal bend, you can ride spirals to make your circles smaller and larger. In addition, asking the horse to alternate which muscles he engages and relaxes serves to gymnasticize the horse. This takes place, for example, in shoulder-in and turn-on-the-forehand when the horse must remain in balance and engage his hindquarters while he simultaneously relaxes over his topline.

Take lots of breaks, reward your horse, and pay attention to the fact that your horse stays motivated and does not get stressed.

3.1 Half-Pirouette with Poles

This exercise motivates the horse to work actively during exercises, such as half-pirouette at walk, turn-on-the-haunches, and turn-on-the-forehand.

What Do I Need?

4 ground poles.

Setting Up

Place the poles along the centerline near X. The distance for trotting poles is approximately 4.25 feet (1.3 m).

How Does This Exercise Work?

(1) Ride up the centerline at a working trot. Trot over the poles, then halt shortly before C or A.

(2) Now, reverse direction by riding a half-pirouette at the walk, a turn-on-the-haunches, or a turn-on-the-forehand. Halt.

(3) Trot on again and trot over the poles. As you approach A or C, halt and again perform a turn, taking care to change the direction of the turn.

(4) Repeat this as often as desired. Take breaks, during which you ride around the whole arena or on a circle. You can also ride over the poles at the trot without stopping to make a turn afterward.

Tip: Work step by step. Make sure to establish a good tempo at the trot over the poles. Concentrate next on the halt. Give clear, but subtle aids. Let your horse stand for a few seconds before you begin the turn. Ride the turn quietly and reward your horse for each step. After your horse completes the 180-degree turn, allow him to stand for a few seconds. Then give him the cue to trot on. From the start, your horse should work actively.

This exercise can also be ridden at the walk.

What Is the Horse Learning?

Concentration. Obedience to the rider's legs. To work actively in exercises such as turn-on-the-forehand and haunches, or half-pirouette.

What is the rider learning?

Coordination of various aids. Refinement of the aids.

What to Do if...?

The horse drifts off the centerline.

In the beginning, don't make this exercise too difficult. Consider positioning additional ground poles or cones along the centerline to help. Check your own aids: sit straight, don't fold at the hip. Frame your horse with your aids on both sides. If needed, work at the walk in the beginning.

My horse rushes through the turns.

Bring a sense of calm to this exercise. Allow your horse to stand for a longer time at the halt and praise him. Trick your horse a bit by ending your turn after only 90 degrees and riding away toward the outside.

3.2 Change Rein across the Diagonal

The exercise "Change Rein across the Diagonal" can be ridden during warm-up at walk and trot. This manner of changing direction is required in many dressage tests. Even at lower levels of competition, this arena figure should be ridden clean. At the higher levels of dressage competition, this change of direction can be used for an extended trot or lengthened trot to demonstrate the horse's movement potential. In any case, ground poles and cones can help provide a good introduction to this exercise for beginner riders or young horses.

What Do I Need?

2 cones, 2 ground poles.

Setting Up

The cones stand in the corners near F and H, several feet from the rail. The ground poles form a passageway at X.

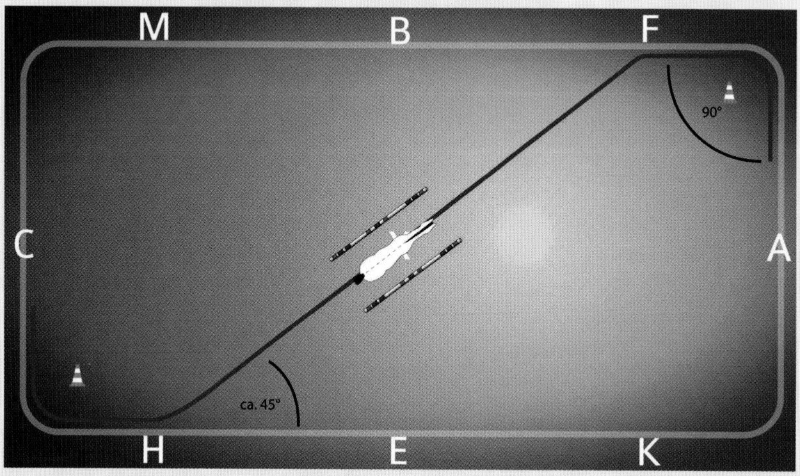

How Does This Exercise Work?

(1) Tracking left, ride the whole arena. On the short side, at C, ride into the corner at H, begin to turn. Ride through the two ground poles. X is, therefore, the center point of the diagonal H-X-F.

(2) At F, return to the track and ride into the corner. Now, you are tracking right.

Variation: This exercise can also be ridden at the canter. At X, you can ride either a simple or flying lead change. Or, ride the simple or flying change just before you reach the track instead. Or, you can continue in counter-canter.

Heads Up! At the posting trot, don't forget to change your posting diagonal about one horse-length before you reach the track in the new direction. Ride into the corner correctly, avoid turning it into a half-volte.

Looking ahead through the horse's ears makes it easier to arrive at the track with precision.

Aids: To ride through the corner, ride straight into the corner and shorten your tempo. (Build positive muscular engagement through your body and your horse's and think about the imminent turn.) Don't pull on the reins! Bend the horse around the inside leg, so that the horse is lightly positioned to the inside (inside rein). Shift your weight onto your inside seat bone and follow this by driving with the inside leg. Complete the corner this way and then ride straight for a short bit before you turn at H and ride straight across the diagonal. The turn at H is about 45 degrees. (Pay attention to the activity of the hindquarters during this turn.)

On the diagonal, the horse is pointed straight ahead. Frame the horse with your aids on both sides. There should be an even contact on both reins and your weight should be evenly distributed on both seat bones. Drive your horse "good and forward" while he's crossing the diagonal. At F, return to the track and ride through the corner (as described above). (The inside rein positions the horse to the inside, while the regulating outside rein sets a boundary. The inside leg aid drives, the inside seat bone is weighted, muscles engage throughout the body—the horse bends around the inside leg.) →

→ 3.2 Change Rein across the Diagonal

What Is the Horse Learning?

Paying attention to the rider's aids. Bending and going straight.

What Is the Rider Learning?

Riding with precision. Forward-looking, proactive riding. Initiation and effects of positive engagement (tone) throughout the body: what does engaging my body do? How do I use increased tone purposefully? Riding through the corners. Straightness. Correct repositioning of the horse.

What to Do if...?

My horse does not reach the targeted point.

Double check that you are applying your aids as described above. Look ahead to the point where you wish to arrive. Turn your upper body with your gaze. Drive with your legs. Pay attention to the aids that provide outside boundaries and frame your horse.

The turn off the rail doesn't work.

Ride the corner cleanly—if your horse is not traveling into the corner, drive more firmly with your inside leg, sending the horse toward your outside rein. (A careful, short tap with the whip on the shoulder can help here in difficult cases.) Then, ride in a pleasant arc onto the diagonal. If you're finding it difficult to turn onto the diagonal, imagine that you want to ride a volte, beginning at the point where you want to turn. If your horse already knows the exercise and wants to anticipate, then turn your horse as expected but actually ride a volte before you go across the diagonal.

Moving straight across the diagonal is difficult.

Double check that you are applying your aids as described above. Weight your seat bones evenly. Drive with your legs. Ride at an energetic tempo, which will make it easier for your horse to stay straight. Do not use your reins to correct your horse's drifting. There should be an even contact on both reins, and the rider's hand always stays soft.

Variation: In between the poles, halt, back up, side-pass over the ground poles and in front of the ground poles, and other creative ideas.

3.3 Simple Serpentines

Simple Serpentines is a basic exercise with a good gymnastic effect. When ridden with correct positioning and bend, you can loosen up the neck muscles of your horse. This exercise develops the horse's concentration and activates the hindquarters. The Simple Serpentine is ridden in various dressage tests, usually at the trot. This exercise lays the foundation for the lesson *Leg-Yield from the Rail and Back* (see *Exercise 6.5*) and is a good way to test out your horse's connection and straightness.

What Do I Need?

2 cones, 2 ground poles.

Setting Up

The cones are positioned in the corner before M and just after F. The poles lie somewhere between 13–19.5 feet (4–6 m) away from the rail.

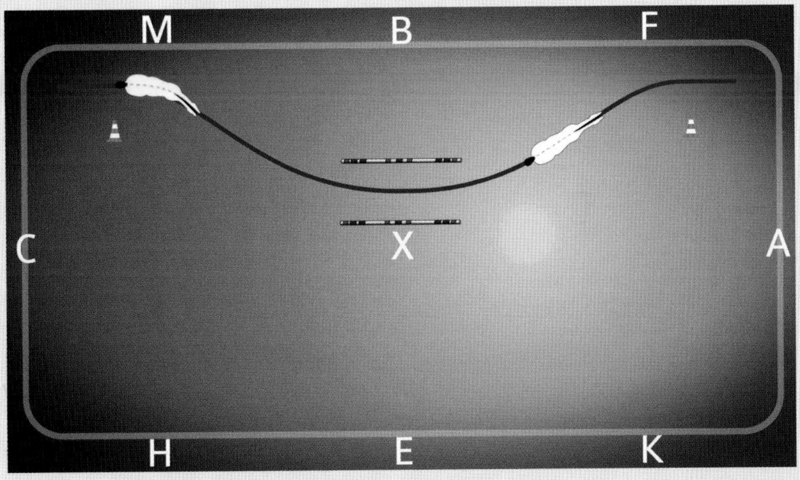

How Does This Exercise Work?

(1) Ride at the walk or trot (in posting trot, you will need to change your diagonal twice). After the corner, turn away from the rail. Ride the corner with the horse positioned and bending to the inside.

(2) After you turn away from the rail, position the horse so that he looks outside—toward the rail. Ride between the poles. Then, turn again in the direction of the rail. Not until just before you reach the inside track should the horse be repositioned once again. The positioning takes place softly and with flow.

What Is the Horse Learning?

Positioning and bending. Obedience to the leg aids. Promotes concentration. Activates the haunches.

What Is the Rider Learning?

To check on connection and straightness. Precise and forward-looking, proactive riding. Riding through the corners. Riding bending lines in balance. To correctly reposition the horse.

→

What to Do if...?

My horse braces and/or tips his head during repositioning.

Make sure that your horse is moving forward. Ride multiple changes of direction and drive forward from the leg. Don't pull on the reins!

Variation: Double serpentines, serpentines with three or four loops using the whole arena.

3.4 Counter-Flexion on the Circle

With this exercise, you can train your horse to shift more weight onto his haunches. This exercise lends itself especially well for large and awkward horses with long backs.

When riding in counter-flexion (the horse is positioned away from the direction of travel), the horse is receiving many gymnastic benefits. The inside section of the neck muscles are stretched, and the inside shoulder loosens up. The outside hind is activated.

What Do I Need?

2 cones.

Setting Up

Position the cones in a straight line, so that you can ride a circle around each cone.

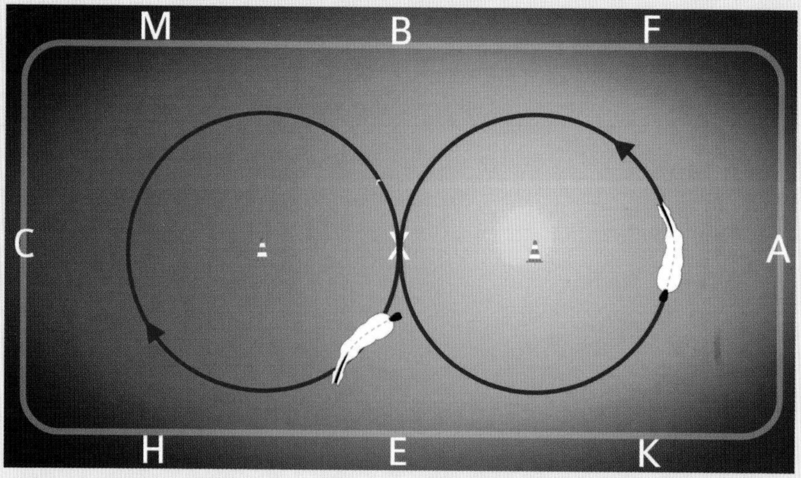

Here, Jessy is training PJ using a subtle opening rein.

How Does This Exercise Work?

(1) At first, ride the exercise in walk or trot. Tracking left, begin by riding a circle around one of the cones. The horse should be positioned left (to the inside).
(2) Now, change to riding a circle around the other cone, forming a figure eight. Do not position the horse, initially. Then, ride this circle with outer, or counter-positioning.

Aids: Use your right (outside) rein to set the direction. Use your left (inside) rein to position the horse. As needed, you can also lift your inside hand about a hand-width higher. Your shoulder should move upward together with your hand. In counter-flexion, the upper body of the rider also turns slightly to the outside. This allows your hips to follow →

more effectively. Initially, your weight stays on your right seat bone, so that the horse can follow the rider's weight. Press your left (inside) leg at the girth. The right (outer) leg lies in a guarding position on the horse's side.

Tip: Only change direction once the horse is stable in his positioning to the inside of the circle.

What Is the Horse Learning?

To shift weight to his hindquarters. Increased flexibility. To loosen up the shoulder. More ground-covering stride. Attention to the aids of the rider.

What Is the Rider Learning?

A feel for the shoulder and haunches covering more ground. Riding in counter-flexion.

Variation 1: During the change of direction, you can allow the horse to cross with his forelegs and, by doing so, increase the difficulty of this exercise. To do it, you must also drive with your outside leg.
Variation 2: Ride both circles in counter-flexion. In this way, you can practice repositioning your horse at the point where you change direction.
Variation 3: Changing tempo: (see Exercise 7.4) Ride around the cone in counter-flexion at the walk. Change direction, and as you do so, pick up a trot at the point where you change. Don't ride a second circle—instead ride the whole arena. The horse is set up to carry himself better into the trot. You can also train the upward transition from trot to canter. The horse will carry himself more on the hindquarters as he picks up canter. As more is required of the horse's outside hind leg, it makes for a stronger departure into canter from that leg.
Note: This variation is especially good for horses that tend to run into the canter or bolt.

What to Do if...?

My horse tilts at the poll and continues to move straight ahead.

Make sure that you are not only positioning the horse with your inside rein, but are also giving an aid from your inside leg.

Heads Up: It's important that during this entire exercise the forward impulsion is never lost. The horse should not stand still under any circumstance.

My circles get smaller and smaller throughout the exercise.

You are turning your upper body too sharply in the turn. Think more about the line of the circle.

3.5 Spiraling In on a Circle

With this exercise, you are training correct positioning of the horse to the inside. The horse shifts more weight onto his haunches and trains the muscles for correct longitudinal bend.

What Do I Need?

1 cone.

Setting Up

Stand the cone in the center of a circle.

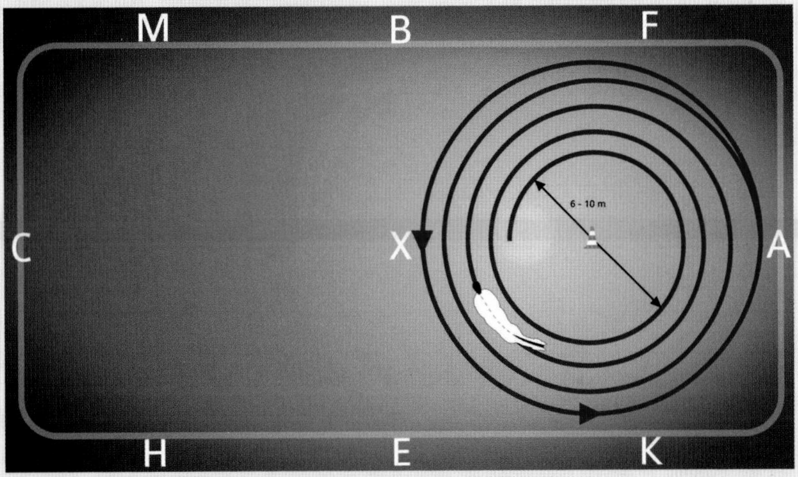

How Does This Exercise Work?

(1) You can ride this exercise at all three gaits. First, ride it at the walk, later in trot, then finally at the canter. Ride once or twice around on a circle. Round by round, make your circle smaller, spiraling in.

(2) When your circle becomes the size of a volte, begin to make it larger again until you are back to your original line of travel on your largest circle. Then, ride the whole arena or another ring figure to promote relaxation in your horse.

Heads Up! Make sure that the line of your circle stays even and does not become egg-shaped. Altogether, it should take you five circle rounds to turn your larger circle into a volte. The smaller the circle, the more difficult it is for the horse. As mentioned in the Introduction (see p. 2), for the inexperienced, the diameter of the volte should never be smaller than 10 meters; for more experienced horses and riders, it can be as small as a 6-meter circle. The smaller the circle gets, the more your inside leg must drive.

(3) Ride the exercise in both directions in order to evenly strengthen the muscles on both sides.

What Is the Horse Learning?

To shift weight onto the hindquarters. Longitudinal bend and positioning to the inside. Obedience to the leg aids.

→

→ 3.5 Spiraling In on a Circle

To spiral in on the circle, Quintano must clearly shift more weight onto his hind leg.

What Is the Rider Learning?

To correctly position the horse to the inside. Forward-looking, proactive riding. Refinement of the aids.

What to Do if...?

My horse falls to the inside.

Check your aids. Drive more strongly with your inside leg aid and less with your outside leg. Don't pull with your inside rein. Put less weight on your inside seat bone.

My horse won't spiral in.

Check your aids. Make a point of riding several feet away from the track more frequently if your horse does not like to come off the rail. Frame your horse with your aids.

3.6 Shoulder-In and Turn-on-the-Forehand

Here, the horse learns to coordinate and cross his legs. This exercise develops balance and activates the haunches.

What Do I Need?

2 cones, 4 ground poles.

Setting Up

Position the cones on the centerline at a distance of about 32–39 feet (10–12 m) from one another. The poles lie along the quarterlines to form an "alleyway."

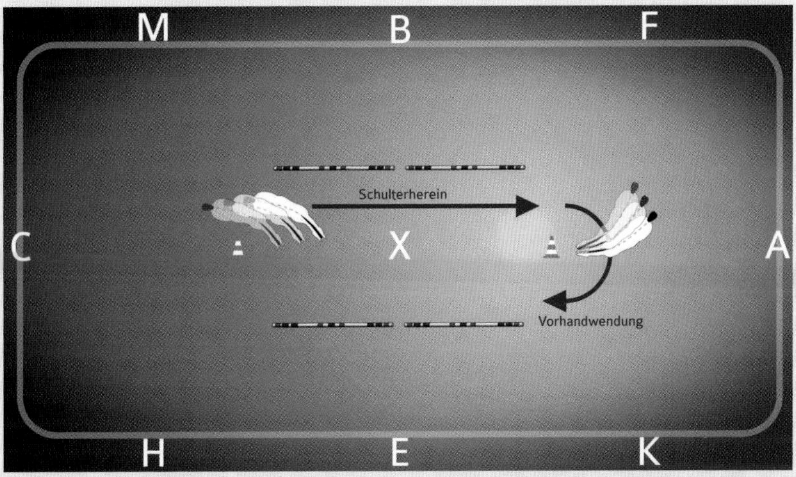

How Does This Exercise Work?

(1) Ride near the centerline at a walk. Near a cone, begin to ride shoulder-in and then continue to ride ahead in shoulder-in to the second cone. Halt once you are even with the second cone.

(2) Now, begin a turn—similar to a turn-on-the-forehand but moving around the cone. Depending upon where you have positioned yourself in relation to the cone, the horse must not only move his hind end but also his forelegs. You have executed a 180-degree turn. Now begin with shoulder-in on the other side of the centerline.

(3) Take breaks, ride the whole arena and change rein. You can also practice the shoulder-in at the trot.

Aids: Shift your weight to your inside seat bone in order to facilitate the horse bringing his inside hind farther under the center of gravity (tracking-up). Imagine that you are about to begin a volte, and use your inside leg aid at the girth to encourage the horse to bend. The inside rein positions the horse and the outside rein restricts his shoulder, in order to lift it. The outside leg lies in place, regulating/guarding.

What Is the Horse Learning?

To pay attention and develop concentration. To step up under the center of gravity. Balance in lateral movements. This exercise promotes bending, positioning, rideability, total willing cooperation.

→

The inside hind leg reaches farther under the center of gravity, and the outside shoulder lifts.

Tip: This exercise is helpful for horses who pace at the walk. It encourages the topline to relax so that they can again find a rhythmic walk. In this case, ride the shoulder-in on four tracks.

What Is the Rider Learning?

Coordination and refinement of the aids. A feel for lateral movements.

What to Do if...?

During shoulder-in, my horse gets too close to the centerline.

As a guide, place two additional poles on the centerline. Frame your horse better with your aids. Check to make sure you have enough contact on the outside rein to control any sideways movement.

Some riders try to use their inside rein to get the shoulder-in. This only serves to pull the horse's head toward the center of the ring. The actual goal—to free up and lighten the outside shoulder—cannot be reached in this way as the horse simply falls more onto that outside shoulder. Imagine, you want to ride the first step of a volte.

My horse loses rhythm.

Remember to support your horse's outside hind with your outside leg.

First practice the shoulder-in on the rail, then on a circle. When your horse can maintain his rhythm for a longer stretch, practice again using the long side of the arena, several feet off the rail, without the help of a boundary on the outside.

3.7 Backing through Slalom

What Do I Need?

3 cones.

Setting Up

Position the cones at a distance of about 6 feet (2 m) apart for "rookies," about 3 feet (1 meter) for "novices," and 1.5 feet (.5 meter) for "the pros."

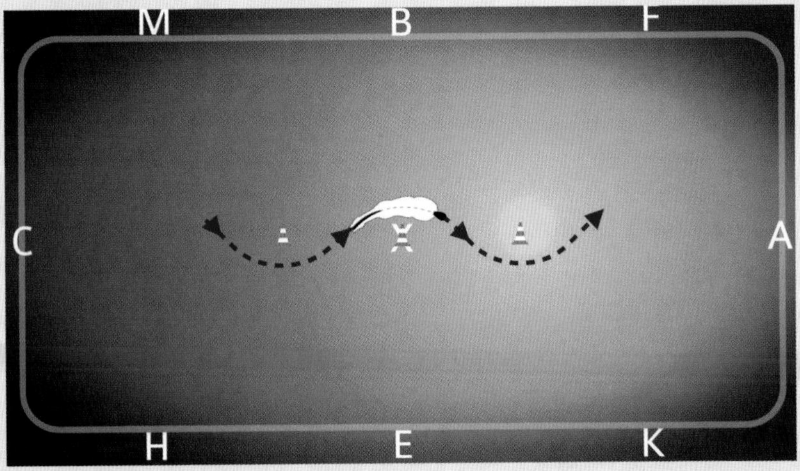

How Does This Exercise Work?

Ride slalom backward through the cones.

Aids: If you would like to turn your horse to the right, you must position your horse to the left, shift your weight to the left and apply the regular aids for backing-up.

What Is the Horse Learning?

Trust. Softening to the weight aids and reins.

What Is the Rider Learning?

Trust. Correct aids. Body awareness.

Heads Up! Pause often, praise your horse, make sure the horse stays motivated and does not become stressed.

What to Do if...?

My horse always takes very big strides all at once.

Ride the turns with flow, and as soon as the horse stands and turns, his haunches should move more laterally.

My horse does not want to back up.

Practice backing up as described in Exercise 4.2.

Tip: For the "pros," make sure you are riding this exercise in an almost straight line, so that the horse bends well off your shifting weight aids and light positioning.

Tip: Only look around when your horse is standing—not when he is stepping backward—so that you don't inadvertently affect the weight aids. Certainly, you can also strengthen the influence of your seat by turning with your upper body.

4. Rhythm

The horse's rhythm and his mental and physical relaxation and suppleness are directly related to one another. If he is not relaxed, elastic, and supple, the horse cannot improve his rhythm.

The rhythm should be symmetrical, regular, and ground-covering. Rhythm and the ability to cover ground can be improved in the following ways:

At the Walk: The movement of the rider's hips describes a horizontal figure eight. As such, the right and left hip alternate when they move forward. At the same moment, the hip moves forward on a certain side, give the rein on that side. (For example, your left hip moves forward, at the same time your left hand gives on the rein—and the opposite applies to the right side). To help get you started, bring your elbows closer to your body. Then, while working on a long rein, allow your whole forearm to move forward with your hip on the same side. The horse will cover more ground, his shoulder will free up, and his back swings.

At the Trot: Ride forward at the posting trot with your horse working in a forward and downward "stretchy" frame. Regulate the trot using an even posting rhythm. The horse should adapt to your rhythm. Make sure that your upper thigh and knee are not gripping and that your lower legs find your horse's sides. When you desire an easy trot, keep your posting low and sit deeply in the saddle. If you need your horse to move forward more energetically, make the rise of your post more energetic.

When working on a bending line, you can also deliberately post on the "incorrect" diagonal, which helps you to support the horse's inside hind leg at the optimal moment.

4.1 On a Long Rein (Every Gait)

When the rider's hand is too strong and the horse's back gets tight as a result, it can disturb his rhythm. In this exercise, the horse should learn to relax and find his rhythm when being ridden forward and downward in a stretchy frame, with his nose ahead of the vertical.

How Does This Exercise Work?

Using both the whole arena and circles, ride your horse on a loose rein at all three gaits.

Tip: Maintain a following seat at the sitting trot and canter and post the trot at first. Your horse needs a balanced, quiet rider who uses seat and leg aids to guide him.

Aids: Rhythmically drive your horse forward. By doing so, you'll help your horse to move forward with relaxation and suppleness, meaning the hind end engages actively and he swings through his back. Sending your horse forward is especially important with horses who get quick, as doing so helps such horses regulate.

Sit straight with your upper body and remain relaxed and balanced. Allow yourself to be carried, without inhibiting the horse.

Freddy enjoys being given a long rein.

In the exercise, the opening rein is very important. Turn with the horse and show him the way, that is, allow your inside hand to come far to the inside. Allow your outside hand to follow in the same direction—as far as the roots of the mane on the horse's outside.

What Is the Horse Learning?

The horse is learning to carry himself, balance, and gain trust for the rider's hands. This exercise develops correct muscling over the topline and encourages the horse to respond to subtle aids.

What Is the Rider Learning?

To ride without relying on the reins. She learns to ride with weight, leg, and lighter rein aids, as well as plan and look ahead proactively. Through this exercise, the rider learns how a horse feels when he is carrying himself with relaxation and suppleness, thereby, making his gaits easier to sit.

> **Tip:** The moment your horse's tempo increases without you asking, ride multiple voltes. Drive your horse clearly forward as you do so, and sit deeply in the saddle.

What to Do if...?

My horse runs, out of control.

> Turn your horse onto a bending line using your opening rein (and leg and seat aids). Stay on the bending line until the horse has become steadier again (the stretching of back muscles on the outside of his body will often help calm the horse). Then transition to the walk.

I get anxious at the canter.

> Look for a helper who can work with you on the longe line. Slowly let out your reins. Your helper should not send the horse forward or even really pull on the longe line. Just by you sending him forward, your horse will become more comfortable to sit and also steadier.

Practice riding this exercise for at least four weeks, without riding any other exercises with contact. You will see how lightly the horse will come to respond to you and how amazing a refined communication between human and horse can be.

What Errors Can Happen?

The fold at the hip: Avoid this by opening your shoulders and imagining that you want to present someone with a vase full of flowers, carried in front of you. Plan where you're going and look ahead, always one-quarter to halfway around the arena or circle you're riding.

4.2 The Rein-Back (Backing-Up Straight with Poles)

Backing-up is a way of testing the horse's willing cooperation. Lowering and flexing through the haunches is activated by backing-up, then trotting off. Backing has a two-beat rhythm. The horse's legs move in diagonal pairs, as at the trot, but without a moment of suspension.

During the exercise, the horse's croup is lowered and his head is slightly in front of vertical. The back is lightly lifted.

What Do I Need?

1–2 ground poles.

Setting Up

Position the poles 3–4 feet (1 m) from the rail, so that the rail becomes the outer boundary. Use both poles to form a passageway. You can also practice this exercise outside of the arena (substituting a pasture fence or similar for the outside boundary).

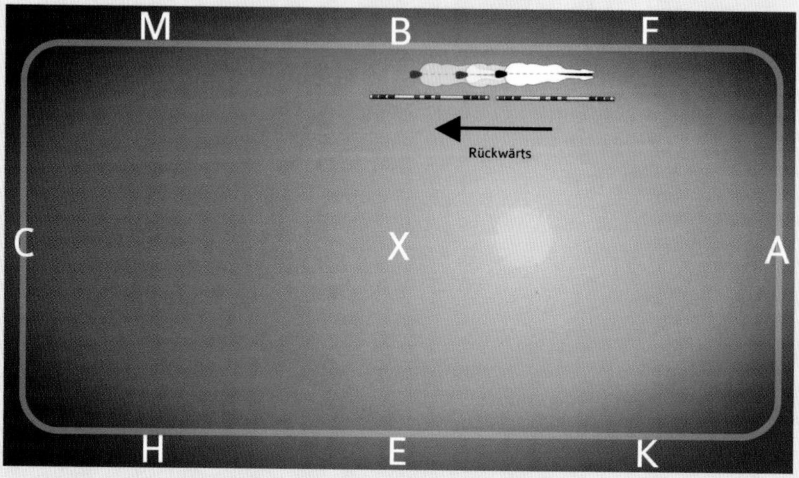

Tip: Your horse should already know this exercise well through groundwork. As you introduce it, remain calm and praise small successes. Praise your horse as soon as he accepts your aids.

Note

Horses often resist this exercise because:

(1) It's difficult for the horse to lift through the back and step backward at the same time while balancing the weight of the rider.

(2) In nature, backing-up is a sign of withdrawal and meekness. It is, therefore, a sign of submission.

Tip: In the beginning, don't attempt to back up more than one horse-length. More than 6–8 steps can cause the horse to interpret this as a fight.

Often, in Western riding, both rein and leg aids are only applied as a brief (rather than a constant) pulse—that is, the release of the aids rewards the horse for responding correctly.

How Does This Exercise Work?

1) First, give the signal to walk on. Through a regulating rein aid (lightly holding against both reins), redirect the impulse to move forward so the horse is stepping backward. You use the same driving aids whether moving forward or backward.

Aids: As you give the aid to move forward, bring your lower legs back into a guarding position. The weight shifts onto the seat bones. If your horse wants to walk forward, take up both reins lightly, redirecting the impulse to move forward. The rider's upper body folds slightly forward.

Heads Up: Don't pull, tug, or haul on the reins! Don't topple forward.

Tip: Set an exact intention for how many steps you want the horse to back up. In the beginning, give after every step and praise your horse.

→

→ 4.2 The Rein-Back (Backing-Up Straight with Poles)

What Is the Horse Learning?

To flex the joints of the hind legs. Attentiveness.

What Is the Rider Learning?

Correct aids. Refinement of the aids.

What to Do if...?

My horse moves at an angle when he backs up.

Practice backing-up with clear boundaries in place. When you halt, make sure the horse is standing straight. Apply your aids equally on both sides.

My horse backs in a 4-beat rhythm.

Apply the inside leg and outside rein more strongly (and the outside leg and inside rein, respectively). By doing so, you are signaling him to move his legs in diagonal pairs.

My horse raises his head above the contact.

Work on your connection before you practice the rein-back. At the halt, position the horse a little bit deeper. Maintain a light positioning to the inside. Don't pull on the reins. Take your time.

My horse stands still/won't back up.

Practice from the ground.

My horse hurries as he backs up.

Most often a tense back is the root cause. Ride long, bending lines, encouraging the horse to move forward and swing through his back.

My horse backs up more steps than I've asked him to.

Insufficient obedience is the root cause here. Increase your horse's attentiveness with exercises such as shoulder-in (*Exercise 3.6* and *Exercise 7.1* can also provide a solution).

My horse spreads his hind legs as he backs.

If the distance between the hind legs is wider than the distance between the fore-legs, it's a balance issue. Before practicing further with backing-up, do some more work on balancing exercises (see *Exercise 4.1*).

My horse drops through his back and lifts his head up.

The source of this problem is with the rider: Don't ride with rough, high, or hard hands.

My horse over-flexes at the poll.

The rider's hands are hard. Using your leg, drive your horse to the bit.

4.3 Canter Departure from Volte

This exercise is especially good for horses that have difficulty departing into canter, tend to get the incorrect lead (e.g. pick up the left lead when tracking to the right), or run into canter. This exercise trains for a deliberate and harmonious upward departure into canter.

What Do I Need?

1 cone.

Setting Up

Position the cone somewhere between X and a point along the circle.

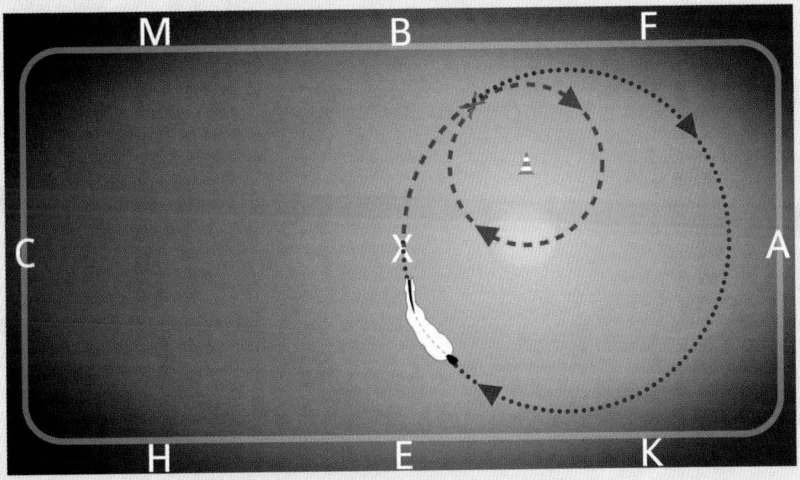

How Does This Exercise Work?

(1) At the trot, ride a volte around the cone. Continue riding the volte at trot until the horse is steady and relaxed.

(2) Then, when you are between B and the cone (see diagram), give your horse the aids to canter and canter farther on the circle.

What Is the Horse Learning?

Orderly departure into the canter on the correct lead. Prevents bolting into the canter. The horse obtains the correct bend for the canter. Hot horses learn to concentrate on the bending line.

What Is the Rider Learning?

How to apply the aids for a correct canter departure. Refinement of the aids.

Heads Up! Stay calm and relaxed. Only ask your horse to canter when he is concentrating on you.

→

Ghost departs willingly into the canter.

What to Do if...?

My horse runs off at a fast trot, but won't canter off.

Go immediately back to riding the volte, until the horse is steady and supple once again. At this steady trot, ride around the cone. Try your canter departure again. In order to heighten the horse's attention to the rider's aids, you can build in lots of transitions. Make sure that the connection with your inside rein—though it's being used for positioning in the volte—is not too tight. Remember to give with your hands over and over again.

The horse departs on the incorrect lead.

Double check that you are not riding your horse with too much positioning to the inside.

As you ask for the canter, make sure you have contact with the outside rein but that your inside rein is allowing.

Variation for Young or Green Horses: Position a cone in the corner between A and K, about 4 feet (1 m) from the rail. You can ride the volte in the corner then ask for the canter departure in the corner. Then, you can canter on using the whole arena. Young horses (as well as nervous horses) do better with this variation as they are not overwhelmed by having to find the guiding line on the circle.

4.4 Lifting the Back

During this exercise, your horse's stride will become noticeably more ground-covering, so that he begins lifting through his back in the loin area. This exercise improves connection.

What Do I Need?

A boundary line or an arena wall. You can use 1–2 ground poles to form your boundary line on the ground of the arena if you prefer.

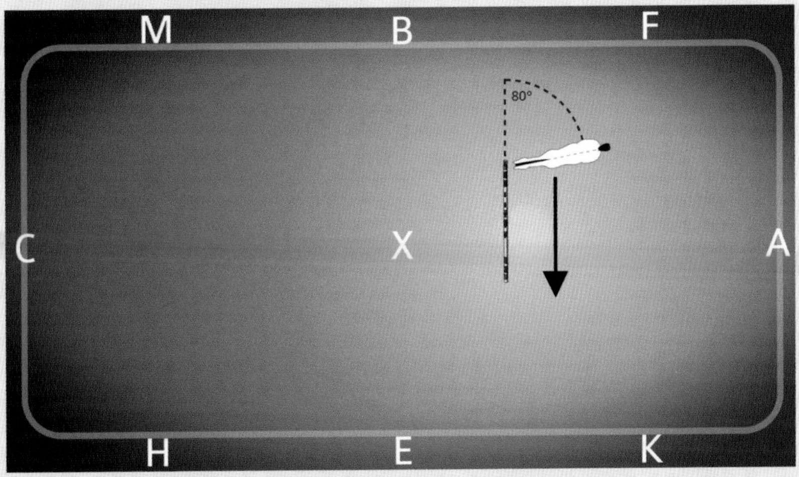

How Does This Exercise Work?

(1) Begin by tracking left at the walk, then ride the horse sideways at an 80-degree angle, facing the arena wall or boundary line. Your horse should not be positioned in either direction.

Aids: Sit straight and direct your gaze toward the track or boundary line. There should be an even, light contact on both reins. Your weight is evenly distributed on both seat bones. The right leg works at the girth, the left lies lightly behind the girth in a guarding position.

(2) As soon as the horse obeys the aids, and clearly steps farther under the center of gravity, stop the exercise by continuing to track left (ride the whole arena on a long rein at any gait).

Tip: Ride this exercise slowly. The exercise is executed correctly when the horse clearly steps up under his center of gravity with the hindquarters. Motivate your horse with praise after a good sideways step. Don't create stress for your horse with this exercise.

What Is the Horse Learning?

To lift through his back. To step up under the center of gravity. To extend at walk, trot, and canter. Increased obedience to leg aids. Correct engagement of the back muscles. →

The horse should clearly bend and cross his hind legs.

What Is the Rider Learning?

A feel for a ground-covering, striding walk, diligent trot and ground-covering canter.

What to Do if...?

My horse barges out through his shoulder.

Increase the contact a bit on the left rein to help regulate the horse's shoulder. To bring the forehand and hindquarters back into line, apply both legs in a guarding position.

My horse resists with his hip and tries to turn.

Apply your right leg more strongly. Don't restrict the horse with your reins.

My horse evades by going backward.

Help your horse to understand that neither the boundary line/arena wall nor your leg aids are dangerous. Begin the exercise again, staying very calm. If it still doesn't work, dismount and try the exercise on the ground.

My horse rushes.

Again, approach the exercise calmly. Start over again and work step by step.

4.5 Counting Canter Strides

Being able to effectively lengthen and shorten your horse's canter strides is important to the execution of many dressage movements, riding patterns, and jumping courses.

With this exercise, you'll get a feel for the length of your horse's canter strides. You'll internalize how it feels when you lengthen or shorten the stride.

What Do I Need?

4 cones, 1 helper on the ground.

Setting Up

Position the four cones an equal distance apart on the line of a circle. Estimate the length of your horse's canter stride and position the cones at that distance from one another.

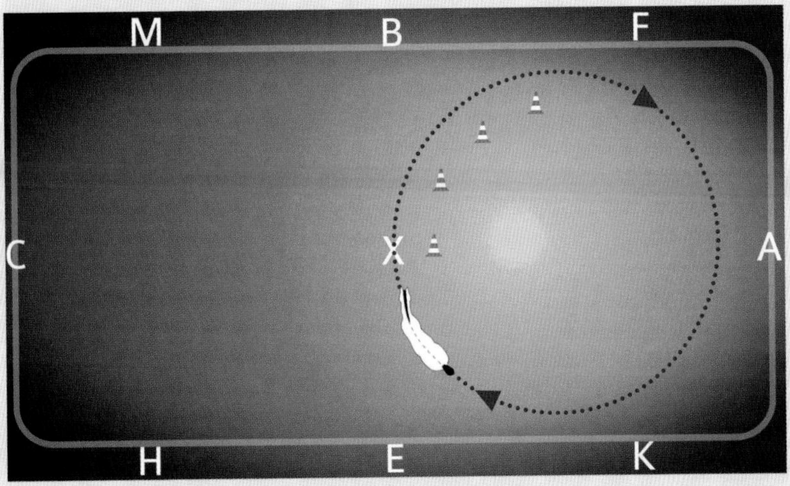

How Does This Exercise Work?

(1) Riding on a circle, canter past the cones. Was your estimation accurate? Your helper can adjust the position of the cones so that the distance between them is the actual length of your horse's canter stride.

(2) Check in with your horse: is every canter stride the same length? Practice riding so that the strides of your canter are even.

Variation: On opposite sides of the circle, position more cones so that they are either closer together or wider apart than the cones that reflect your horse's typical stride length. Now you can practice bringing your horse back at canter or lengthening his canter stride.

What Is the Horse Learning?

To maintain an even basic tempo at canter. To shorten and lengthen his canter strides. To pay attention to the rider's aids. →

→ 4.5 Counting Canter Strides

Begin counting canter strides at the first cone.

What Is the Rider Learning?

To feel the length of canter strides. To maintain an even rhythm. The difference between working canter, collected canter, and medium canter.

What to Do if....

My horse's canter strides vary in length.

Work on your canter. You'll first see improvement here after multiple training sessions. Ride lots of transitions (trot-canter, canter-trot, walk-canter, canter-walk).

Position canter poles: for Western: 6–7 feet (1.8–2.1 m); for dressage and jumping: approx. 10–11 feet (3–3.6 m) around the arena, and do some additional work with cavalletti.

4.6 Trot-Canter Transitions

With this exercise, you'll be training the transition from the trot to the canter. The rhythm of the canter is established and willing cooperation is fostered. You can also practice this exercise at the counter-canter (as opposed to cantering on the "true," or inside, lead).

What Do I Need?
3–4 ground poles.

Setting Up
Position the ground poles for trotting about 3–4 feet (1–1.3 m) apart on the centerline between X and G.

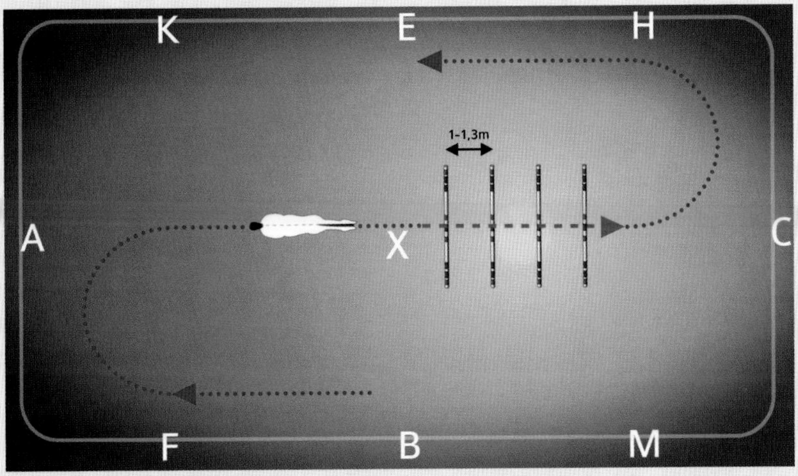

How Does This Exercise Work?

(1) Ride at a canter on the rail. At A, turn up the centerline and ride straight toward the poles. Transition downward to the trot soon enough that you can ride over the poles at the trot. Resume your canter on the same lead and at C continue to canter using the whole arena.

(2) Ride at a canter on the rail. At A, turn up the centerline and transition downward to the trot before you reach the trot poles. After the poles, transition upward to canter on the opposite lead and at C continue to canter using the whole arena, but in the new direction.

(3) Track left. At H, pick up the counter-canter and ride down the long side to K. In the corner, execute a simple change of lead and at A, turn and canter up the centerline. Trot over the ground poles and then transition to canter on whichever lead you desire. At C, turn right or left (in accordance with the true canter lead you've chosen) and ride the entire arena. →

(4) Tracking right, ride at the canter on the rail. At C, ride a tight turn onto the centerline toward the trot poles. Ride over the poles at the trot. After the poles, canter on, turning left at A and turning onto the diagonal at F. When you reach the centerline, transition downward to trot, turn right onto the centerline, and trot over the poles in the opposite direction. At C, return to the rail and continue tracking right.

Aids: Concentrate on each transition. Give clear canter aids. Half-halt and steady the horse in the turns, helping him to balance more weight on his hindquarters. Turn your upper body in the turn and look ahead. Execute a precise transition to the trot ahead of the ground poles.

What Is the Horse Learning?

Concentration. Attention to the rider's aids. Obedience to the leg aids. Changes of lead and counter-canter. Willing cooperation. Rhythm at the canter.

What Is the Rider Learning?

Transitions. Coordination of the aids. Proactive, forward-thinking riding.

What to Do if...?

My horse doesn't transition to the trot in time.

Allow yourself enough time for the transition. Already transition downward to the trot when you are several meters away from the poles. As you progress with this exercise, you can shorten this distance. If needed, you can add in a volte before the poles, during which you transition down to the trot. This can also help with horses who get to "running" at the trot after the downward transition.

A motivated Soraya trots right up the middle of the ground poles. Afterward, continuing forward at canter.

5. Relaxed and Supple

We must distinguish between mental and physical Losgelassenheit (relaxation with suppleness and elasticity). In work, the horse should stay motivated and his mental performance should improve. Excitement and stress lead to psychological tension, which can easily turn into physical tension. Past traumatic experiences can be reversed through trust and correct work under saddle.

Like people, tense horses can become relaxed through the loosening of muscles and fascia, as well as through the release of muscular adhesions (tension knots). Speak with your horse's physiotherapist about possible exercises that you can practice daily with your horse.

A strong application of rein aids, a poorly adjusted cavesson, or a noseband pulled too tightly can also all cause physical tension.

The "squeaky" sheath-noise that male horses sometimes make has its origins in tension. It's caused by extremely tense abdominal muscles. The back muscles are no longer engaged and the horse is trying to complete the requested movement by compensating with his belly muscles.

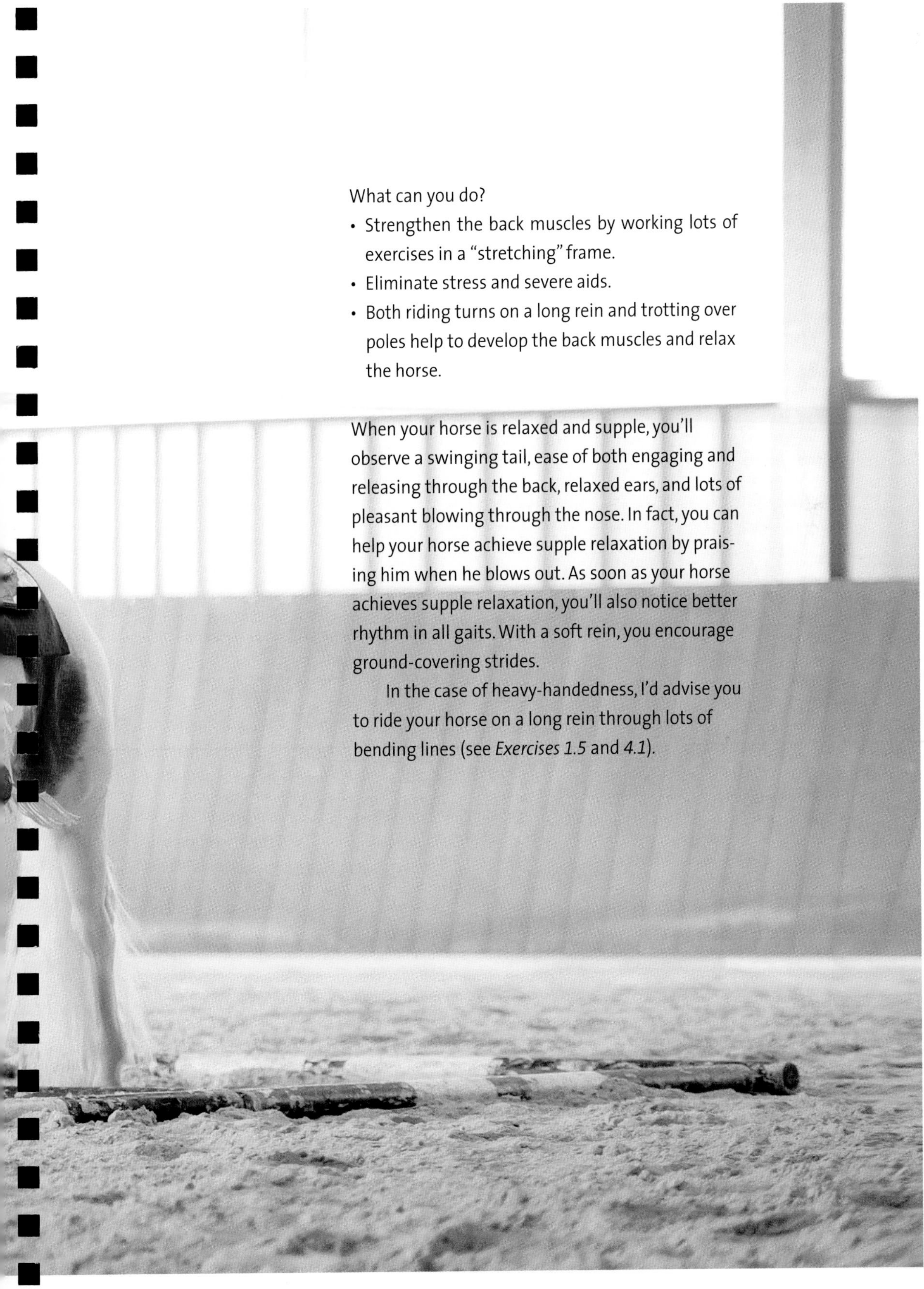

What can you do?

- Strengthen the back muscles by working lots of exercises in a "stretching" frame.
- Eliminate stress and severe aids.
- Both riding turns on a long rein and trotting over poles help to develop the back muscles and relax the horse.

When your horse is relaxed and supple, you'll observe a swinging tail, ease of both engaging and releasing through the back, relaxed ears, and lots of pleasant blowing through the nose. In fact, you can help your horse achieve supple relaxation by praising him when he blows out. As soon as your horse achieves supple relaxation, you'll also notice better rhythm in all gaits. With a soft rein, you encourage ground-covering strides.

In the case of heavy-handedness, I'd advise you to ride your horse on a long rein through lots of bending lines (see *Exercises 1.5* and *4.1*).

5.1 Precise Transitions

To encourage willing cooperation, it is important to ride many transitions, both between and within the gaits. In many types of equestrian competition, clean transitions are highly valued.

Precise Transitions Exercise 1— On the Circle

What Do I Need?

4 ground poles, 4 cones.

Setting Up

Position the ground poles as in the diagram. Place a cone near every pole.

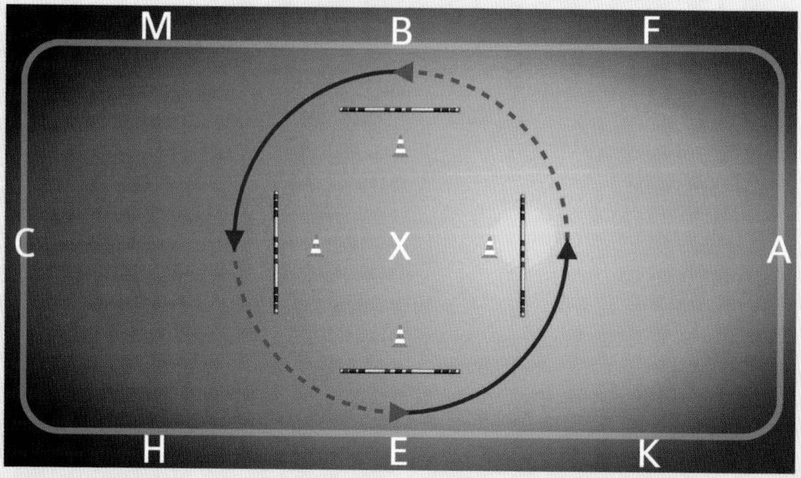

How Does This Exercise Work?

(1) Ride on a circle at the walk. When you are in line with each pole, ride a transition. In the beginning, walk-trot, trot-walk or walk-halt, halt-walk. The poles allow you the possibility to slightly vary the points where you execute the transitions.

(2) Next, you can begin to utilize the cones as your point of orientation. The transition should always take place exactly as the horse's shoulder is in line with the cone.

(3) Build in lots of changes of direction and make sure to ride the exercise on both sides.

Aids: *For a circle tracking left,* position your horse to the inside using your left rein and regulate him on the outside with your right rein. Shift your weight toward the inside and apply your leg aids. Look in the direction that you want to go.

What Is the Horse Learning?

To react with sensitivity to the rider's aids. To activate the hindquarters through changes of gait.

What Is the Rider Learning?

Refinement of the aids. A feel for riding transitions.

What to Do if...?

My horse won't stop.

Sit deeply in the saddle. Keep your legs against the horse's sides.

Heads Up! Don't pull or tug on the reins. Pressure generates counter-pressure! Many horses run against pressure on their mouth. Support your transition with calming voice aids and don't forget to exhale.

My horse gives the minimum when I ask him to trot on.

Give your horse a clear cue. Drive him powerfully forward. Don't accidently block the horse from moving forward by inadvertently having too much rein contact or a tight back.

If your horse doesn't respond, you can support your driving aids by tapping him with your whip. Breathe in deliberately as you do so.

My horse anticipates the transition.

Be careful not to stiffen or brace during the transitions. Occasionally, make sure you return to riding the whole arena or a different ring figure. You can also build in transitions of tempo within a gait (*see 6.1*).

My horse stumbles and is uneven in his rhythm.

Typically, a horse will only stumble when the hindquarters are inactive and the horse is traveling on his forehand. Try to encourage your horse to move forward with more push from behind. Build in exercises such as *Trotting On from Backing Up (Exercise 7.1)*.

Heads Up! Just before stumbling, horses tend to lean against the reins. Ride your transitions so well that you don't need to use the reins at all.

Precise Transitions Exercise 2—Transitions in the Aisle

With this exercise, you'll train downward transitions or a simple change of lead.

What Do I Need?

2 ground poles.

Setting Up

Position the poles like an "alleyway" or "aisle" on either side of X, parallel to the short sides.

How Does This Exercise Work?

(1) Ride on a circle at any gait. As you cross X, execute a transition. The horse should be straight at the point of transition.

(2) Build in a change of direction at this point as well, so you are circling in the new direction. As you come through the aisle, you can change your gait. →

Aids: *For the circle,* position the horse to the inside and use your outside rein to regulate him. Weight your inside seat bone and drive him forward with your legs. Look in the direction that you want to go.

Prepare the horse *for the transition* at least 5 meters ahead of time with a coming together of all the aids, in order to increase the horse's attention. This way, at the desired point of transition, you should only need to apply a light aid in order to change the gait. Here, we're referring to half-halts (see p. 19). Breathe deeply through the belly as you transition to a new gait.

Heads Up! Following every direct application of the rein aids, there must be a release of the rein aids.

Tip: Support the transitions using voice commands that are familiar to your horse. Utilize your breath as an aid: for example, inhale deeply when you want to trot on and exhale as you ask for a downward transition.

In the *change of direction,* pay attention to the positioning of the horse at the point of change. Carefully use your new inside rein to position the horse in the new direction. Regulate the horse on the outside and send him forward. Shift your weight onto your new inside seat bone.

What Is the Horse Learning?

Transitions without depending on the rail. To activate his hindquarters. To respond with sensitivity to the rider's aids.

What Is the Rider Learning?

Correct riding on a circle. Precise transitions between the gaits. To coordinate the aids.

What to Do if...?

My horse anticipates the transitions.

Be sure to incorporate other exercises in between transitions. Ride through the aisle without executing a transition.

My horse halts too late.

Be more specific with your aids. Don't pull on the reins. Try again using voice commands and correct breathing. Practice!

5.2 Serpentines

This exercise can be applied all the way up to riding flying changes at the canter.

What Do I Need?

4 ground poles.

Setting Up

The ground poles are set up in pairs on the centerline, parallel to the short sides of the arena, as aisles (see diagram).

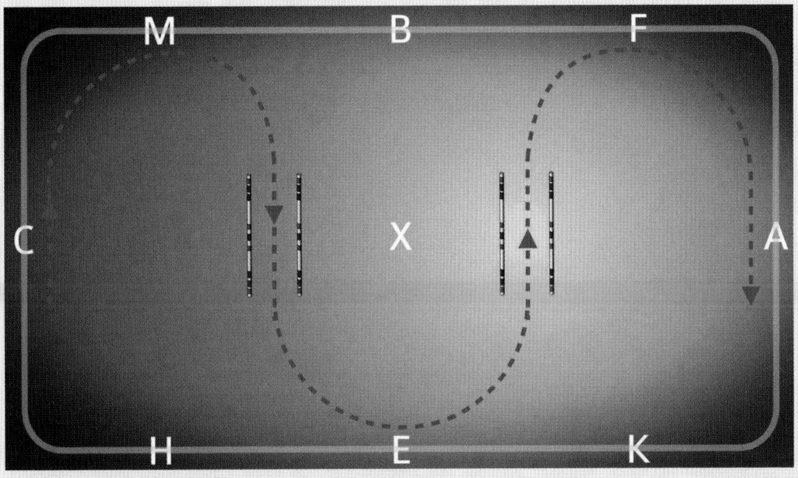

How Does This Exercise Work?

(1) Ride a serpentine with, for example, three loops.

(2) In between the poles, straighten your horse out and build in a transition. For example, ride your serpentine at the trot, but walk in between the poles.

Tip: Give yourself enough time to reposition your horse.

Aids: The serpentine consists of three loops and each loop contains a bending line and a straight line. On the straight lines, frame your horse with your legs and reins while sitting evenly on both seat bones. On the bending line, sit to the inside and drive from the inside while your outer rein regulates the horse's outside body. The inside rein positions the horse while the outside rein sets the boundary.

What Is the Horse Learning?

Correct repositioning through a change of direction from one bent line to another bent line. The (walk-trot) transitions relax the horse. Trot-halt-trot transitions encourage energetic departure. Canter-walk-canter transitions serve as an exercise in collection.

What Is the Rider Learning?

To ride precise transitions. Corrections during changes of direction. Accurate riding. →

What to Do if...?

My horse anticipates the transition.

From time to time, ride this exercise without making a transition in between the ground poles.

My horse pulls against the reins and doesn't want to do the downward transition.

Be light in your aids. Prepare better for the transitions. Praise your horse when he does accept the aids.

Plan your course ahead of time.

Variation: Add three cones to the set up described in this exercise.

What Do I Need?

4 ground poles.

Setting Up

Set up as above adding 3 cones.

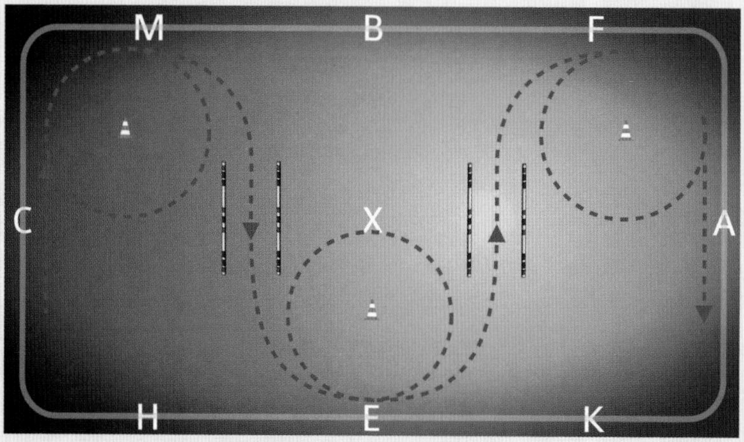

What Is the Horse Learning?

The voltes quiet the horse. Through the additional longitudinal bending and elongation of the muscles on the horse's outside body, you can help the horse achieve mental and physical relaxation with elasticity and suppleness.

What Is the Rider Learning?

The additional voltes help the rider learn to ride even circles and to achieve a forward and downward, stretchy frame with the horse.

What to Do if...?

My horse isn't shortening his canter stride.

Consider what the source of the problem may be: is it possible that his musculature is not yet conditioned enough for this? Revisit *Exercise 4.5, Counting Canter Strides.* Is your horse overwhelmed mentally? Transition to a walk on a long rein. Ride quietly at all three gaits until you have reestablished suppleness and relaxation.

5.3 Double Squares

The double square with ground poles is a great activity for both beginner and advanced riders. This exercise emphasizes how to ride a round volte. In the part of the exercise where you ride straight ahead, you can check whether your horse will travel straight without positioning and whether he is tracking up actively with his hind end.

What Do I Need?

4 ground poles, approximately 10 feet (3 m) in length;
4 ground poles, approximately 6.5 feet (2 m) in length; 1–5 cones.

Setting Up

Position the four shorter ground poles so that they form a closed square. Leaving 3 feet (1 m) in between, position the four longer ground poles parallel to the shorter ones to make a larger square. Leave open space in the corners (see diagram).

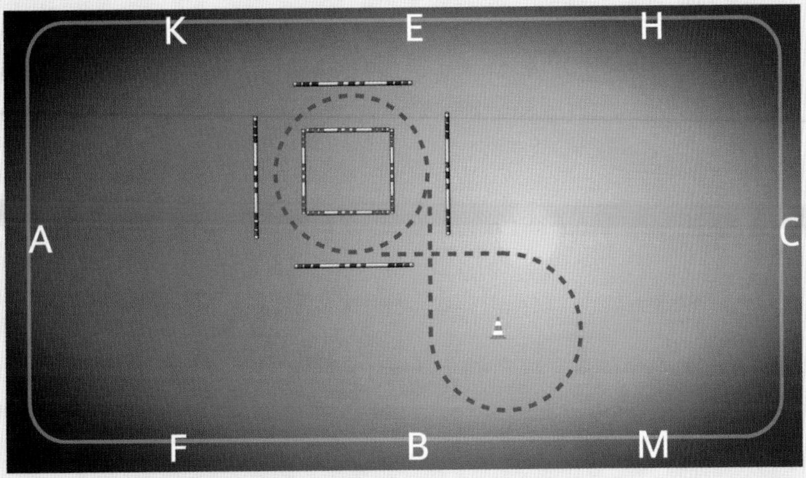

How Does This Exercise Work?

(1) Ride a volte around the small square but within the larger square. Ride at a marching walk.
(2) Using the ground poles as visual boundaries to your right and left, practice straightness by riding through them. As you ride straight ahead, sit up tall and distribute your weight evenly over both seat bones. Drive from both legs to frame the horse. You should have an even contact on both reins.

Aids: When riding the volte, the inside rein positions the horse and the inside leg drives him forward. The outside leg lies in a guarding position on the horse's side. Together with the outside rein, the outside leg sets a boundary for the horse on the outside, preventing him from stepping to the outside of the larger square. Your weight is on the inside seat bone. Look where you're going, toward the next quarter of the volte.

Tip: The smaller the circle, the more important it is for you to look ahead.

Heads Up! If your horse wavers from the line of travel, do not correct him with the reins. Instead, use both calves to strongly drive him forward to the reins. By doing so, present your horse with a clear line of travel. If the horse is stepping up actively behind, it is easier for him to stay straight. →

→ 5.3 Double Squares

What Is the Horse Learning?

The horse learns to move forward and straight, meaning that the forehand and hindquarters are not wavering from his line of travel. Bending and positioning. To take more weight onto his hindquarters. Responsiveness to the rider's aids.

What Is the Rider Learning?

To correctly ride the volte. Training her gaze to divide the volte. Refinement of the aids. Correct bending and positioning in the turn. How to ride a straight line without positioning the horse. To change from positioning on a bending line to riding a straight line without positioning. To frame the horse.

What to Do if...?

The horse barges through the outside shoulder.

Often, the outside regulating (guarding) rein is missing. Take more contact on your outside rein and apply your outside leg more strongly.

My horse always barges to the left, no matter which direction we're traveling.

If a horse always tips to one side, he is likely asymmetrical.

Work hard on the exercises recommended for straightness (see chapter 8).

Double Squares: Variation 1

What Do I Need?

4, 10-foot (3 m) ground poles, 4, 6½-foot (2 m) ground poles, 1 cone.

Setting Up

Position the four shorter ground poles as a closed square. About 3 feet (1 m) away, position the four longer ground poles parallel to the others, forming a square that is open at the corners. Position the cone outside of the squares, so that you can ride a volte around the cone. It should form a figure eight when you ride a volte around the cone in one direction, then change direction and ride a volte around the small square. (Refer to the diagram of the squares on the previous page.)

How Does This Exercise Work?

(1) Inside the larger square, ride a volte around the small square.

(2) Ride at a marching walk. Change rein and ride a volte around the cone. Then, go back inside the square—you're riding a figure eight. You can also ride multiple circles around the cone and then go back to the circle within the square and vice versa.

Heads Up! Pay careful attention to the change of rein in this exercise. Before you reposition your horse, you should ride a few steps straight ahead at the walk (or trot).

What Is the Horse Learning?

Bending and positioning. Correct tracking-up. To shift more weight onto his hindquarters. Responsiveness to the rider's aids. To change between bending and straight lines.

What Is the Rider Learning?

To correctly ride the volte. Looking ahead along the sections of the volte by training her gaze. To refine her aids. Correct bending and positioning in the turn. Correct flexion. To ride straight ahead in between the turns.

Double Squares: Variation 2

What Do I Need?

4, 10-foot (3 m) ground poles, 4, 6½-foot (2 m) ground poles, 4 cones.

Setting Up

Arrange the cones evenly outside the two squares, so that you are able to ride a volte around each cone. It should form a figure eight if you ride a circle around one of the cones and then a circle in the other direction around the small square. (See the diagram on p. 69 for how to set up the squares.) Ideally, the cones should be eight walk strides apart from one another.

How Does This Exercise Work?

(1) Riding on a straight line, enter the square and then ride out through one of the open corners. Now, ride a volte (or two or more) around the nearest cone.

(2) After your volte, ride straight back into the square. On the next open corner, ride out again and ride a volte around the nearest cone. Following this pattern, you can ride a volte around each of the four cones.

Tip: Always change your volte by reentering the squares and riding a volte around the small square in the opposite direction from the volte around the cones.

Heads Up! Position and bend your horse correctly in the volte; ride straight ahead in between the volte.

What Is the Horse Learning?

Change of bend. Positioning and straightness.

What Is the Rider Learning?

To organize the volte into sections. Consistent application of the aids.

Double Squares: Variation 4

What Do I Need?

5 cones.

Setting Up

Leaving four cones in place from the Variation 2 (above), remove the ground poles and position the fifth cone in the center.

How Does This Exercise Work?

Ride as in the previous variation. Here, you won't have the visual aid of boundary lines formed by ground poles.

Tip: Pay attention to the direction of travel and ride large, round voltes.

What to Do if...?

It's difficult for my horse to change flexion so quickly.

> Ride your voltes around the cone twice in the same direction, without straightening the horse immediately after the first time around. Do your best to prepare the horse for the upcoming change of direction (which will be moving straight ahead).

Tip: Don't get too set on correct positioning and bend at first. Instead, make sure that the small circles are round and don't become egg-shaped.

The horse wobbles during the change of direction.

> Make sure that you are riding a few steps going straight ahead, before you attempt positioning in the new direction.

5.4 Zigzag Ground Poles

With this exercise, you can check whether your horse is on the aids. You can use this exercise to train your eye for the most suitable course and practice riding tight turns as well as riding straight and centered over obstacles. You are practicing riding an even serpentine at walk and trot (in combination with voltes).

What Do I Need?

4–6 ground poles.

Setting Up

Position the ground poles in a zigzag pattern along the centerline. The poles should be at 90-degree angles to one another.

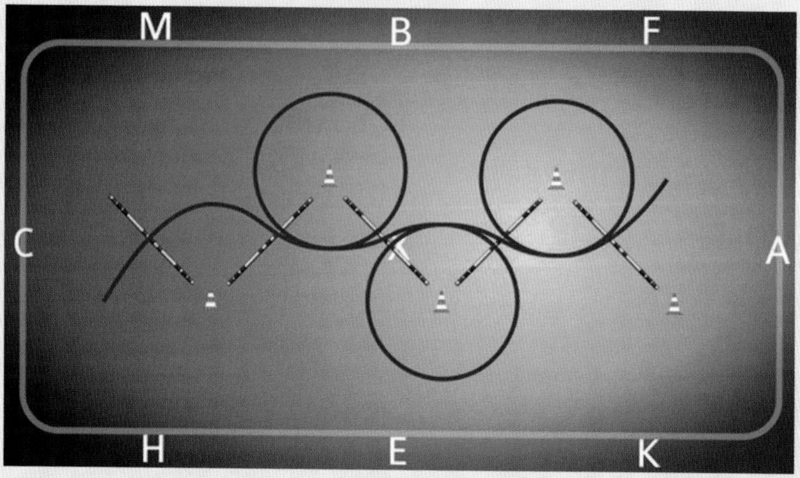

How Does This Exercise Work?

(1) In this exercise, you'll ride a serpentine on the centerline for the length of the arena. Use the ground poles to orient yourself, ride straight and centered over them.
(2) Under no circumstance should you ever work the turns using only your rein aids. Shift your weight as appropriate and drive forward at the same time. Through every loop, position the horse in the direction of travel and through every change of direction, ride a couple of straight steps at the walk/trot.

Tip: Should your horse ever resist flexing in the desired direction, build in a volte, riding the circle until you have achieved the desired positioning.

What Is the Horse Learning?

Bending and flexing through tight turns with regular changes of direction. To react quickly and with flexibility to the rider's aids. Enhanced concentration. Straightness in between the changes of direction.

What Is the Rider Learning?

To look ahead in the turn. Straight and centered riding over obstacles. Bending and positioning/repositioning the horse. How to ride serpentines.

Zigzag Ground Poles: Variation 2

What Do I Need?

4–6 ground poles of equal length, 4–6 cones.

Setting Up

Position the ground poles in a zigzag pattern on the centerline. In each corner formed by the ground poles, place a cone (see diagram p. 72).

How Does This Exercise Work?

(1) Begin by riding a serpentine up the centerline. Ride straight and centered over the poles.

(2) Next, add in a volte around the cones. Ride a circle! Half of the volte is defined by the poles. Ride the second half of the circle in accordance with the first—make it even and round. Position the horse in the direction of the turn with the help of your weight aids. Drive the horse forward throughout the exercise in order to make sure he continues to work with his hindquarters.

(3) As you change direction, ride a couple of straight steps at the walk/trot.

What Is the Horse Learning?

Bending, flexion, and repositioning. Straightness and to track up strongly from behind.

What Is the Rider Learning?

To divide the volte and train the gaze accordingly. Refinement of the aids. Bending and positioning. To ride both straight lines and serpentines.

What to Do if...?

My horse is barging through his shoulder.

> Stay consistent with your aids. Double-check that your outside rein is not hanging. Position your outside leg in a guarding position on the horse's side and send him forward.
>
> **Tip**: If you find you need to set a further boundary on the horse's outside body, you can use a short crop on the horse's outside shoulder.

We don't make it over the middle of the poles.

> Check your aids: Did you already have your goal in sight as you rode the prior turn? Are you looking sufficiently ahead? Are you distributing your weight as appropriate during the turns? Is either rein hanging? Or, are you holding too hard on both reins? Where are your legs positioned?

During the change of direction over the poles, my horse begins to get crooked.

> The changes of direction are too sudden for the horse—remember that you must include a step or two of straight walk or trot before you ask the horse for flexion in the new direction. Weight both seat bones evenly and maintain an even contact on both reins. Drive the horse forward sufficiently so that he tracks up with his hind legs.

The loops of my serpentine are uneven.

> Look ahead and give clear aids. Make this exercise a regular part of your daily schooling.
>
> **Tip:** Position the ground poles close to a boundary (the arena wall or fence) and/or position more poles or cones as guides to the sections of the exercise.

5.5 Figure Eight

This exercise not only trains the rider's eye for riding large circles more evenly, but also helps the horse to engage his inside hind more correctly through the bend, shifting more weight onto his hindquarters. As you reposition the horse through the change of direction, you will ride over the ground pole positioned in the center. This helps the horse lift his shoulder as he changes flexion and activates the hindquarters, requiring the horse to bend more through the joints of his hind legs. This exercise also helps horses that tend to get quick and rush, to become calmer, and it has good gymnastic effects.

What Do I Need?

2 cones, 1 ground pole.

Setting Up

Position the cones at a distance of about 32 feet (10 m) apart. In the middle of the two cones, position the ground pole.

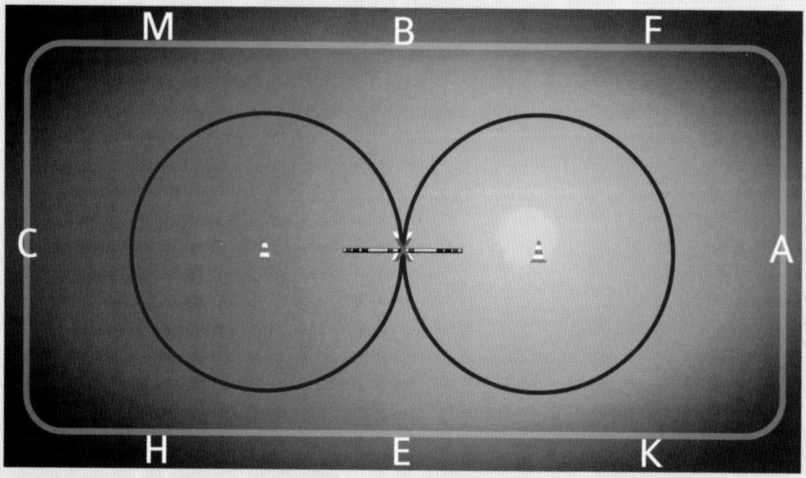

How Does This Exercise Work?

(1) Working at walk or trot, ride a figure eight, forming two even circles around the two cones.
(2) Ride over the ground pole at the point of directional change at the walk or trot. As you do so, ride straight ahead for one horse-length, then reposition your horse as you track in the new direction.

Aids: Working in either direction, position your horse on the circle using your inside rein and drive him forward from your inside leg. Use regulating outside rein and leg aids to prevent the horse from drifting outward on your circle.

Tip: Always look ahead, directing your gaze toward the arena wall or fence. Don't look in the direction of the cone or at the ground. At the point where you change direction, make sure to ride the horse straight for a couple of strides and then carefully change his flexion.

What Is the Horse Learning?

Correct, even bend, and circles. Activation of the hindquarters. The horse learns to lift his shoulder through changes of direction, and to respond to the rider's seat aids with sensitivity through the turn.

(Diagram to the left)
Imagine the cone stretches up to the sky or use a jump standard in place of a cone here. Your gaze should never be directed downward toward the cone.

(Photo to the right)
Beppo stretches his topline through the turn, which fosters relaxation.

What Is the Rider Learning?

Proactive riding. To ride a circle correctly. To develop a feel for an active hindquarters. Refinement of the aids.

What to Do if...?

I don't reach the ground pole because my horse pushes toward the outside.

Either a clear boundary is not being set by the outside rein and leg aids, or the horse is falling onto his outside shoulder and cannot bend correctly through his back. This exercise is golden for a horse with these issues! Position your cones a little farther apart. For now, your horse may just need to do this exercise on larger circles.

My horse gets quicker and quicker.

Reassure the horse with your voice. As you post, make sure to rise slowly and sit distinctly. Try the exercise without the ground pole. Circle two to three times in one direction before you build in a change of direction, giving your horse time to come up off the forehand and thereby slow down. Praise your horse when this occurs.

In one direction, my horse drifts to the outside, and in the other direction, he drifts to the inside.

Here, your horse's asymmetry is becoming unmistakably clear. Use your leg aids and your regulating rein aid to help him maintain the radius of the circle and be happy with your horse even when he makes small improvements. If this doesn't get better over several schooling sessions, you should seek the advice of an equine body work practitioner or veterinarian. This problem can also originate up above. Perhaps your hips aren't level?

6. Contact and Softness

The Third Step on the Training Scales Is Contact (Classical) and Softness (Western).

With the support of a driving leg, the horse can move into a steady, soft, and elastic contact with the rider's hands. This is also referred to as connection. In Western riding, the rider does not seek a steady contact with the horse's mouth, but rather that the horse should yield easily to the seat, leg, and rein aids.

Caution: Please don't misunderstand "contact" by just pulling on your reins until the horse drops his head! Through resistance and scissoring (pulling back and forth on the reins), the rider can block the horse's back and, thereby, also the hindquarters. In these instances, the horse responds by working against the rider, leaning on the bit, avoiding through his back and either resisting with the muscles on the underside of his neck, or falling behind the vertical.

The rider's hands should wait (and stay soft while they're doing it!) and the leg should drive the horse forward. Only when this sequence is happening correctly can the horse truly move onto the bit. Therefore, I've included exercises known for the development of contact/softness and for activating the hindquarters/impulsion, discussing these topics together in chapters 6 and 7. The exercises each have a different emphasis.

Heads Up! As soon as you run into any of the following common errors of contact, it's a sign that either your horse or your riding hands are not yet ready for the given exercise.

Errors in Contact

1. The horse is behind the vertical.

By applying rein aids too strongly, the rider has influenced the horse to drop the plumb line that runs from his forehead to his nose behind the vertical.

Correction: Bring your hands forward as you apply your driving aids.

2. The horse is entirely behind the bridle.

Now the horse totally avoids the rider's rein aids, instead evading them by bringing his nose far back toward his chest.

Correction: You must reestablish the horse's trust in the rider's hand. Ride on a long rein (see *Exercise 4.1*) and ride definitely forward. Under no circumstance should you attempt to "lift" the horse up by carrying your hands higher.

3. The horse has a false bend in the neck.

By pulling backward on the rein, the rider has tried to force the contact. Now, the highest point of the horse's neck is no longer at the poll, right in between his ears. Instead, the highest point is back farther, about the height of the third or fourth vertebrae of the neck.

Correction: This is difficult to correct. Move forward, keeping your hands very elastic. Frequently allow the horse to "chew the reins out of your hands." The horse must learn to stretch through his topline.

4. The horse leans on the reins.

The horse leans on the reins and is not willing to step up enough from behind.

Correction: Activate the horse's hind legs by driving him forward more. Take up the contact and then give appropriately afterward. Ride frequent transitions with sensitive hands. At all costs, avoid hanging onto the horse's mouth for balance.

5. The horse runs away from the reins.

The line from the horse's forehead to nose is well in front of the vertical. The horse braces through his back and pushes upward from the underside of his neck. Over time, incorrect musculature develops.

Correction: Longe the horse, first with long side-reins then later adjusted progressively shorter as he becomes physically capable to carry himself. Ride many loosening exercises (long bending lines; multiple changes of direction; chewing the reins out of the hand). The horse must be encouraged to let go and swing through his back. The best way to inspire your horse to lower his head is through the use of the opening rein.

Please prepare your horse for contact by working with the exercises in chapter 4 (most importantly *4.1*) and chapter 5.

6.1 Cone Game

By riding leg-yields and voltes in this exercise, you can encourage the horse to lift through the back, lowering and activating his hindquarters. This prepares the horse for collection exercises and allows the horse to come more fully onto the aids.

What Do I Need?

6–9 cones.

Setting Up

Set up the cones so there is room to ride a complete volte around each one.

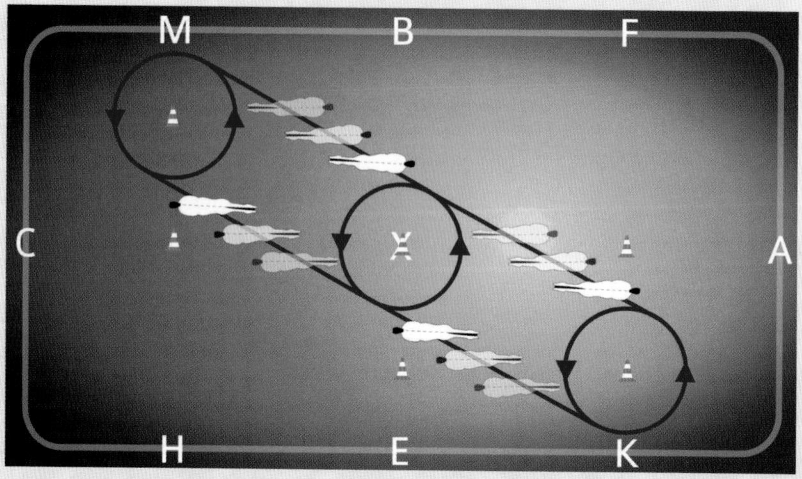

How Does This Exercise Work?

This exercise is divided into various levels of difficulty. The following goes for every level: Ride a volte around a cone. Leg-yield the horse to the next cone, then ride a volte around it.

(1) Four Cones: Begin by riding a volte around the cone at K. Leg-yield the horse to the cone at X. There, ride a volte around the cone. Then, continue riding straight ahead to the next cone, at G. Ride one-and-a-half voltes around this cone. Next, leg-yield toward the cone at E. There, ride a volte and then go straight back to the cone at K. There, you can begin the exercise again.

(2) Three Cones: Ride a volte around the cone near M. Leg-yield the horse to the cone at X. Ride a volte around this cone, then leg-yield the horse again to the cone at K. Here, ride one-and-a-half voltes and then leg-yield back to the cone at X. Ride a volte around the cone at X, then leg-yield the horse again to the cone at M, with which you began.
Do the exercise in the opposite direction, using the following letters: H – X – F – X – H.

(3) Five Cones: Begin with a volte around the cone at G. Leg-yield your horse to the cone at E. Ride a volte and then leg-yield to the cone at D. Ride a volte around this cone and then leg-yield to X. You've now executed a change of direction. Ride a circle around the cone at X and then leg-yield the horse to the cone at M.

Aids: For the *volte*, use your inside rein to position the horse to the inside. Take contact on the outside rein at the same time, in order to prevent your horse from drifting to the outside. Weight your inside seat bone and turn your upper body in the direction of travel. Look where you want to go. Drive the horse from your inside leg and use your outside leg to frame the horse.

For the *leg-yield,* position your horse lightly to the inside, using your outside rein to regulate the horse's outside shoulder. Your weight should be on your inside seat bone. Your inside leg is applied at the girth, while your outside leg should be positioned slightly behind the girth to prevent the horse from drifting out. Look where you want to ride.

What Is the Horse Learning?

To lift through his back. Obedience to the leg aids. To increasingly lower and shift weight onto the hind end. The horse learns to move forward into the leg-yield, with more ground-covering strides.

What Is the Rider Learning?

Spatial planning. Coordination. To both engage the tone in her body and let it go.

What to Do if...?

My horse does not arrive at the correct cone.

> Look ahead and plan your path. Push with your pelvis to point your horse in the direction you want to go. Frame the horse with your outside rein and leg. Drive him forward to your hands.

My circles vary in size.

> Practice riding just the volte. As you do so, you'll become more confident about what an even volte looks like.

6.2 Trotting Poles

With this exercise, you can practice riding straight ahead without a visual border, activate the hindquarters of the horse, and check your seat.

What Do I Need?

4 ground poles, 2 cones.

Setting Up

Position the poles a little off the rail, and the cones along the middle line between A and C.

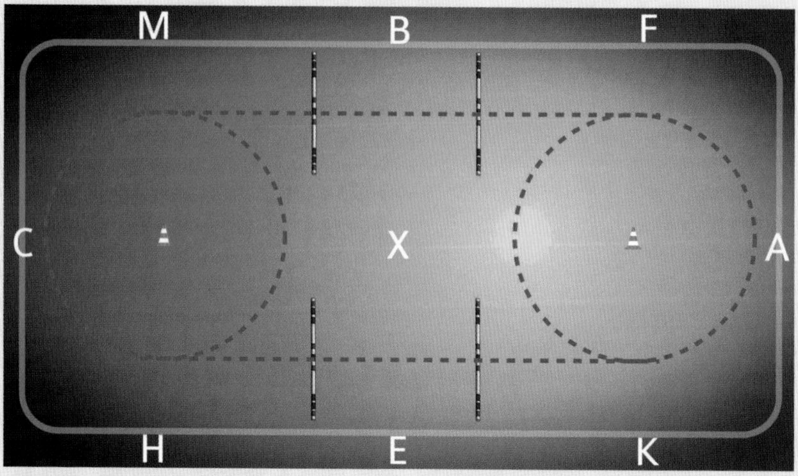

How Does This Exercise Work?

(1) Ride over the poles at the trot and then ride a volte around the cones on the short sides. Begin in posting trot. Trot over the center of the poles. Your weight should be distributed evenly over both seat bones. On the straight lines, use your aids (even reins, driving evenly forward from both legs) to frame the horse.

(2) After the second pole, ride a volte around the cone. The distance to the cones should always be the same on both sides. Your horse will get slower, but he should continue to track up under the center of gravity. As applicable, position your horse to the left or right. So long as your horse also trots readily forward through the turns, you can also sit the trot during this part of the exercise. If your horse maintains an even tempo, you can even sit this entire exercise.

Heads Up: Check your seat. If your hips do not swing with the horse correctly, changes of rhythm can occur and the horse may stumble over the ground poles. Swing with your hips, not your belly.

What Is the Horse Learning?

To move straight without a visual boundary. To negotiate the ground poles and judge distances.

What Is the Rider Learning?

Forward-looking, proactive, and straight riding using the correct aids. The rider learns to allow her hips to swing with the horse at the trot.

What to Do if...?

My horse travels to the outside of the pole and misses them.

Plan your path, ride proactively. Pay attention to the outer boundary that your aids provide the horse (outside rein and outside leg).

My horse gets quicker in the turn.

It may be that your horse is not yet truly balanced. Practice riding through tighter turns (see *Exercise 5.6*).

My horse is not bent correctly.

Remain on the volte until the horse bends correctly around your leg. Only then, try riding the entire exercise again.

6.3 The Diamond (Three Variations)

With this exercise, you are practicing riding voltes and tight turns. You can build in changes of direction and transitions, encouraging willing cooperation in the horse. Diverse possibilities for working over the ground poles and around the cones foster motivation and concentration in horse and rider.

What Do I Need?

4 cones, 4 ground poles.

Setting Up

In the middle of the riding arena, position the ground poles in a diamond shape. Place a cone in each corner of the diamond. Begin with about 3–6 feet (1–2 m) distance between the ends of the poles.

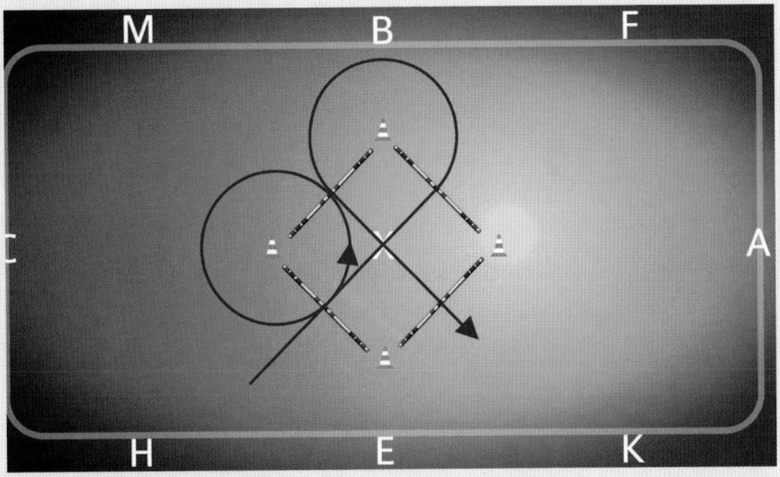

How Does This Exercise Work?

Ride this exercise at walk or trot.

(1) **Volte:** Use the mid-point of the diamond as the start of your volte. The cone is the center of the volte. Always ride over middle of the ground poles, in order to keep your circle evenly round. →

→ 6.3 The Diamond (Three Variations)

Always ride over the center of the ground poles.

Tip: Don't look down at the ground pole or cone. Turn your upper body in the direction of travel, as if you are looking toward an extension of the cone that reaches eye level. (For more on voltes, see ch. 5.)

(2) **Transitions:** Ride straight over the center of the ground pole, changing your gait in the center of the diamond. Continue riding over the middle of the next ground pole, out of the diamond. (More on *Precise Transitions* in *Exercise 5.1.*)
(3) **Changes of Direction:** Riding from M to K, "Change rein across the diagonal." Then, in turn, do the same from F to H (or the other way around). As you do so, ride through the middle of the diamond, crossing over the ground poles on the diagonal. (More on *Changing Rein* in *Exercise 3.2.*)

What Is the Horse Learning?

Bending with correct positioning. Improvement of the gaits. Responsiveness to the aids. Activation of the hindquarters through practice with ground poles. Willing cooperation.

What Is the Rider Learning?

Voltes and tight turns. Transitions and changes of direction. Proactive, forward-looking riding. Refinement of the aids.

What to Do if...?

My horse trips with his forefeet.

Your horse's shoulder is still hanging through the turn. Ride exercises such as *5.6, 5.5, 3.4* and *2.1* in order to lift his shoulder. Make sure that the horse's hindquarters stay active throughout.

6.4 Leg-Yields with Transitions

As the horse crosses his hind legs, he lifts his back. The inside hind steps farther beneath the center of gravity and, thereby, supports a lively upward transition into trot. Because he's tracking up the horse comes more onto the bit, and when the leg-yield is executed correctly, he will also be more on the aids overall. This additional thrust during the upward transition to trot can make it easier for the horse to move forward onto the bit.

Tip: Does your horse move against the reins or bring his head up during transitions? If so, this is exactly the exercise you need!

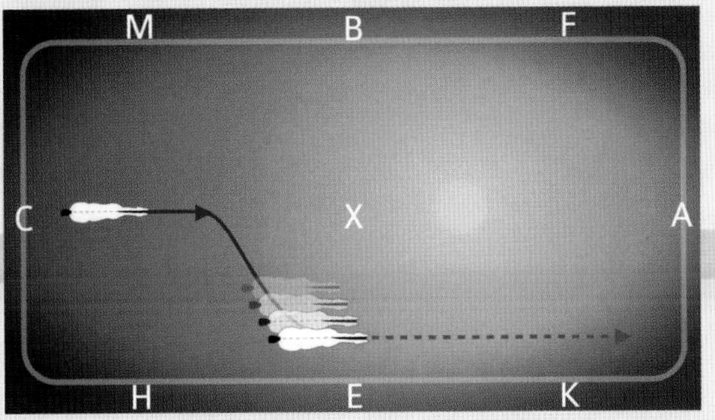

How Does This Exercise Work?

(1) Ride up the centerline and begin a leg-yield toward the rail—let's say tracking right at the walk.
(2) When you are still several feet from the rail, pick up a trot and move straight ahead, coming out of the leg-yield as you trot straight ahead.

Aids: Depending on your riding discipline, you should either weight your inside seat bone or both seat bones. The inside leg sends the horse sideways. The outside (guarding) leg prevents him from falling to the outside. The inside rein positions the horse, while the outside rein regulates his outside body.

What Is the Horse Learning?

Through the leg-yield, the horse learns to step up under the center of gravity and lift through the shoulder. Thereby, he moves onto the bit more easily or even begins to carry himself more through the transitions.

What Is the Rider Learning?

The feel and timing for correct connection/softness. The rider learns to correctly prepare the horse for a transition.

What to Do if...?

My horse pushes against my inside leg and won't step sideways.

Do some groundwork to practice stepping sideways and gently use your outside rein to show your horse what to do. By applying the Three Point Rule (p. 19), you can also support this effort with the whip.

My horse runs toward the rail and takes giant crossing steps.

Your horse has learned really well how to move sideways, but he is getting quick and stepping wide in order to avoid tracking up under the center of gravity. So, the horse is moving sideways but is losing his rhythm and the activity of his hindquarters. Regulate the horse with your outside aids and ride more quietly, in general.

My horse will not transition to trot or canter.

Apply the Three Point Rule (see p. 19) to check in with your horse's responsiveness to the leg aids.

6.5 Leg-Yield from the Rail and Back

This exercise is great for improving the horse's obedience to the leg aids and teaches the rider to regulate the horse using the outside rein. Before tackling this exercise, your horse should already know how to leg-yield (see *Exercise 6.4*).

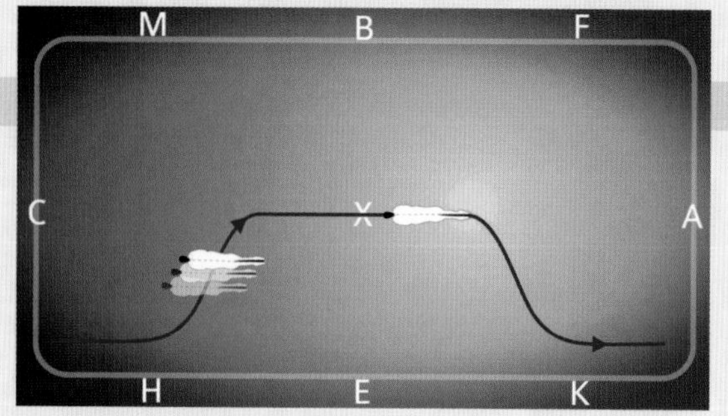

How Does This Exercise Work?

(1) The path you follow resembles the line of a simple serpentine. Track left at walk or trot. Ride through the corner between C and H.

(2) After you pass H, begin to move forward and sideways toward the centerline.

Aids: Position the horse to the right and shift your weight onto your right seat bone. Drive more from your right leg. Take contact on the left rein and position your left leg in a guarding position, behind the girth. By doing so, you'll prevent the horse from getting ahead of his front legs with his hindquarters.

(3) Keeping the horse parallel to the rail, ride toward the centerline until the horse is about 16 feet (5 m) from the rail (or, as an alternative, ride all the way to the centerline as in the diagram). When you are even with E and B, walk (or trot) straight ahead for a few strides. Position the horse to the left. By the time you reach K, the horse should be back on the rail.

What Is the Horse Learning?

This exercise increases willing cooperation. To cross with his legs. Responsiveness.

What Is the Rider Learning?

Refinement of the aids. How the aids work together.

What to Do if...?

My horse's haunches get ahead of his forehand.

Bring your leg that is applying the forward and sideways leg aid farther forward on the girth. The outside, guarding leg should lie behind the girth to limit the horse. The outside rein may give a bit, for example, by opening out to the side. This shows the horse the possibility of moving sideways with his forehand.

We just don't make it back to the rail in time.

The source of the problem is your spatial orientation. Use cones to mark the section where you should ride straight ahead and where you want to arrive at the rail. Begin to practice this exercise with small distances: at first, coming about 3 feet (1 m) off the rail, then 6 feet (2 m), and so on.

My horse's forehand gets ahead of his hindquarters.

Bring your leg that is applying the forward and sideways leg aid back farther. Apply your guarding leg at the girth to limit the horse. Take a light contact on the outside rein.

6.6 Crossing the Street

In this exercise, you are schooling bending and positioning, riding turns, transitions, and straightness with active hindquarters. Using this arena setup, you may also ride this exercise at different tempos, depending on your level (for faster tempos, the ground poles and cones must be positioned farther apart from one another).

What Do I Need?
4 cones, 4 ground poles.

Setting Up
Referring to the diagram, position the ground poles and cones. Leave a distance of about 4 feet (1.2 m) between the cones and poles.

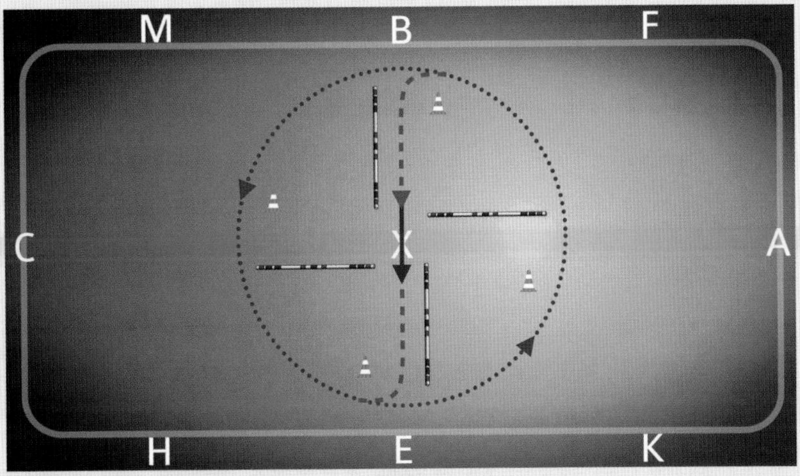

Diagram 1

How Does This Exercise Work?

(1) Begin by riding this exercise at the walk. Ride directly into the arena setup, then straight out. Ride halfway around the circle, then reenter the arena setup (diagram 1). Change direction at the center point.
(2) Look for different ways to ride through this configuration (diagrams 2 and 3). Select specific points where you will execute transitions (at the cones, for example).

Tip: Plan ahead! Think through the course you are going to take through the arena setup and then look in the direction that you want to go.

Heads Up! As you execute transitions, don't forget to send your horse forward even as he shifts into a slower gait. Keep the connection.

What Is the Horse Learning?

Increased obedience. To actively step under the center of gravity. Transitions between the gaits.

What Is the Rider Learning?

Bending and positioning in turns. Straightness and how to straighten the horse. Refinement of the riding aids. Transitions between the gaits.

→

What to Do if...?

My horse shifts and falls out with his hindquarters.

Don't ride from your reins, but rather from your body. Repeatedly ride a large circle around the entire configuration so that you can double check that the bend, positioning, and active tracking up with the hindquarters remain consistent.

My horse rushes through the transition.

Vary your course through this arena setup. Keep the horse busy. Avoid riding the transitions too close together.

As the exercise progresses, my horse gets more and more lazy.

Incorporate large circles.

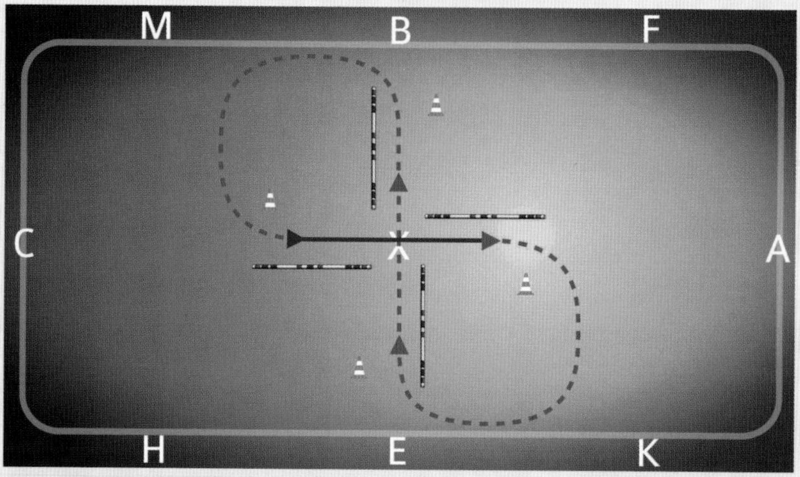

Diagram 2

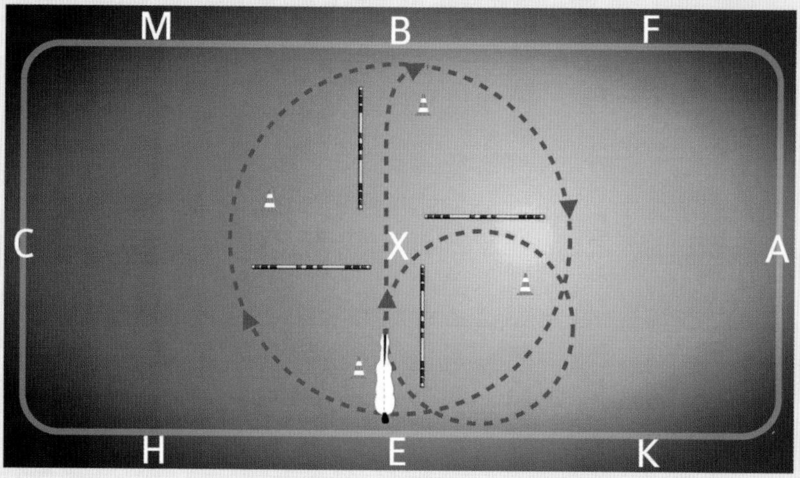

Diagram 3

In this exercise, the rider learns to frame the horse with her aids.

7. Impulsion or Activating the Hindquarters

The fourth step on the Training Scales is Impulsion (Classical) and Activating the Hindquarters (Western).

Contact requires that horses actively track up under their center of gravity with their hind legs. In Classical riding, thrust is developed through energetic, forward riding, which is later converted to increased carrying ability of the hindquarters. When a horse moves with supple relaxation and thrust, it will be comfortable for the rider to sit his gaits because he "carries the rider with him" as he goes. The movement is soft and harmonious.

The impulse to move comes from the horse's hindquarters, which propel the horse forward energetically and direct his movement forward and upward. The horse's trot/canter should be getting bigger and higher. Thereby, the horse gives the impression that he is moving uphill.

Note: Impulsion is the energetic transfer of power from the hindquarters into forward, uphill movement.

For a Western horse, active hindquarters allow him to turn in the smallest possible space, to shoot forward from a standstill, and to stay balanced while carrying his rider at a slow tempo. This dynamic must be fostered at both the trot and canter.

In Classical riding, impulsion is primarily developed at the trot. In Western riding, active hindquarters are often developed at the canter/lope through work on circles, lateral movements, rein-back, or rollbacks, so that the horse learns to lift through his back and take more weight onto his hindquarters.

7.1 Trotting On from Rein-Back

This exercise not only trains the horse to halt at a specific point and back up, but also to actively step under with his hind legs, and execute transitions. In order for the horse to move and lift through his back, which enables him to carry the rider's weight more optimally, he must shift weight off his forehand, back onto his hindquarters. An upward transition from rein-back into the trot is required in many dressage tests.

What Do I Need?

2 ground poles, 2 cones.

Setting Up

Position the ground poles parallel to one another, 3–5 feet (1–1.5 m) apart, along the diagonal from K–M. The poles should be placed in the second half of the diagonal. Position the cones at the end of the poles near M (see diagram).

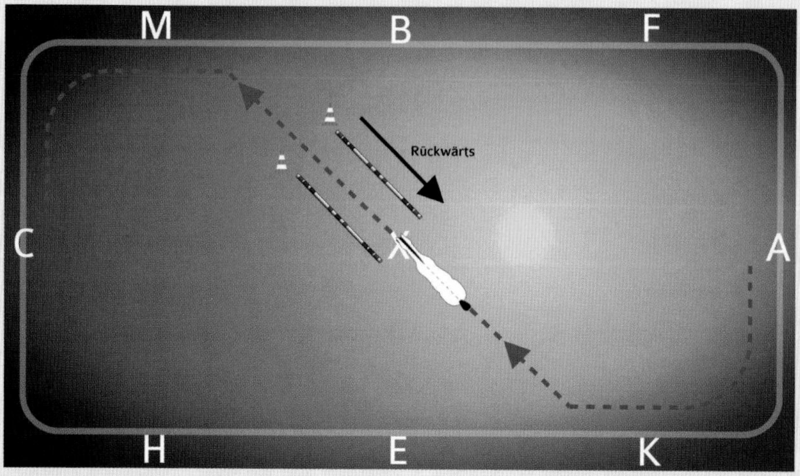

How Does This Exercise Work?

(1) At the trot, change rein across the diagonal, riding through both poles. From the trot, come to a halt between the two cones.
(2) Back your horse a few strides in between the poles. When you reach the end of the poles, trot forward out of your rein-back and complete your change of rein across the diagonal.
(3) Afterward, ride at a posting trot all the way around the arena.

Heads Up! Make sure that your horse backs up slowly and then trots off with energy and power. There should not be any steps of walk in between the rein-back and the upward transition to trot.

What Is the Horse Learning?

A straight rein-back. To halt from the trot at a specific point. To activate his hindquarters. Obedience. Transitions.

What Is the Rider Learning?

The rein-back. To halt from the trot at a specific point. Transitions.

In the upward transition to trot, Bijou's hind-quarters move up actively under his center of gravity.

What to Do if...?

My horse doesn't halt between the cones.

> Solidify your trot—make a halt transition in a different spot, possibly along the rail. Be patient and practice lots of transitions.

The horse halts too soon.

> When an exercise is repeated many times, the horse often comes to anticipate the commands. Outsmart your horse by riding through the poles at the trot a few times, without transitioning to a halt or backing up.

My horse does not stand quietly.

> Practice standing quietly along the arena rail, either when mounted or from the ground. Remain calm and patient. Only begin to ride on again after the horse has stood quietly. Praise your horse using a quiet voice.

Heads Up! Pay attention to your seat! Maintain straightness in your upper body. Don't tip backward as you execute the halt or forward when you ask for the trot.

Note: Using this arena setup, you can also school the side-pass (see *Exercise 10.4*).

7.2 Extended Trot from Shoulder-In

This exercise combines the shoulder-in with riding straight ahead at the trot. In shoulder-in, the horse's inside hind tracks up more definitely under his center of gravity and he loads and flexes his haunches. This improves the carrying power of the hind legs. As you trot straight forward, the hindquarters are activated and impulsion is fostered. The horse develops a floating, ground-covering trot.

How Does This Exercise Work?

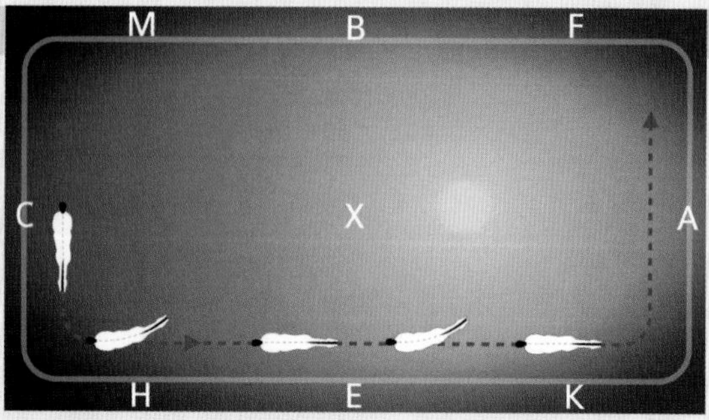

(1) Ride a few steps of shoulder-in at the trot. At some point, trot forward out of the shoulder-in. As you do so, the horse will clearly shift more weight onto his hindquarters and develop more thrust while in motion.

(2) After a short time, resume shoulder-in as you come out of a corner onto the long side.

Aids: Weight your inside seat bone, which enables the horse to more pronouncedly step up under the center of gravity with his inside hind. Imagine you want to begin riding a volte, so apply your inside leg at the girth to ask the horse to bend. Your inside rein positions the horse and the outside rein regulates and lifts his shoulder. The outside leg is in a guarding position.

(3) Before E or B respectively, choose a specific point where you will trot straight ahead. Here, send the horse forward from both legs. Have an even contact on both reins and distribute your weight evenly on both seat bones. Your hope here is that the hindquarters work harder than usual. If after a few steps, you lose this extra power from behind, return to the shoulder-in and return to the forward trot after just a few steps of shoulder-in, as described above. This time, try to maintain the forward, driving trot until you reach the next short side. Then repeat the exercise.

Tip: Time your change from shoulder-in to forward-moving trot to correspond with the moment when the horse's inside hind leaves the ground. This way, the momentum carries forward into the straight movement.

Variation: You can also practice this exercise while crossing the diagonal. To do so, ride through the corner in shoulder-in and then straighten and extend your trot as you come across the diagonal.

After shoulder-in, horses move from behind more actively.

What Is the Horse Learning?

To activate his hindquarters. To actively track up under the center of gravity. To cover ground at the trot.

What Is the Rider Learning?

The rider develops feel for a more active hindquarters (impulsion and thrust). Changing of the aids between a lateral and forward movement.

What to Do if...?

My horse's trot lacks impulsion.

This can be caused by a muscular problem. If your veterinarian says all is in order, take a step back: ride changes of tempo along the arena rail. Ride transitions between and within the gaits. Only after doing some more preliminary work should you try this exercise again.

My horse shoots forward.

Consider the quality of your horse's movement during the shoulder-in. If your horse is not on the aids, the source of the problem has already begun during the shoulder-in. Try the forward trot again once your horse is clearly on the aids during shoulder-in. Please make sure that you are driving the horse forward to the bridle at all times, ensuring a refined connection with the horse's mouth.

If the rider's inside heel comes up, it can cause her weight to slide to the outside, which blocks her inside hip from following or influencing the movement of the horse.

Imagine you want to lift your outside shoulder and, at the same time, touch the arena floor with your inside heel. As you do so, please also allow your inner shoulder to lift.

Tip: The rider's shoulders are parallel to the horse's shoulders; the rider's hips are parallel to the horse's hips.

7.3 Extended Trot from Volte

On a volte, the horse learns clearly how to track up under his center of gravity with his inside hind leg. This helps the horse to lengthen, covering more ground during the extended trot.

What Do I Need?
1–2 cones.

Setting Up
In two corners, position each of the cones about 15 feet (5 m) from the short side and 16 feet from the long side.

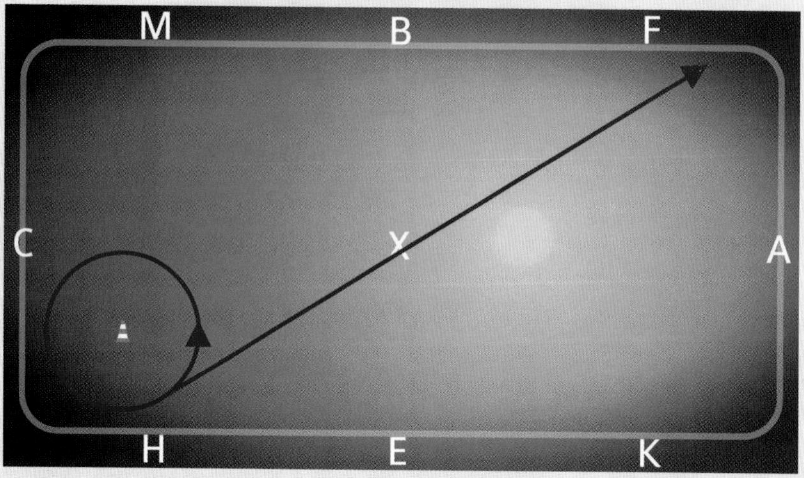

How Does This Exercise Work?

(1) In the corner, ride a volte at the trot.
(2) As you exit the volte, ride across the long diagonal, extending the trot as you do so.

> **Tip:** If the horse loses thrust halfway through the diagonal, you can build in another volte. Only take the horse back once you have reached the rail, so that he doesn't just decide to change the tempo of his own accord before you reach the rail.

Aids: As you leave the rail after the volte, drive your horse forward from both legs. Allow your horse to come forward onto the bridle. In the beginning, do this at the posting trot so that you don't disturb his movement.

> **Tip:** Western riders, this is a great exercise for reining! Ride your volte at a jog, but stand up in a light seat as you leave the rail. Allowing the horse to move forward, you may keep a light contact on the reins. You may also hold on to the saddle horn.

What Is the Horse Learning?

The development of thrust. To actively step up with his hindquarters. To cover more ground. This exercise trains and develops the horse's back muscles.

Alicia drives her horse softly forward into the extended trot.

What Is the Rider Learning?

To ride through changes in tempo. To ride the horse clearly forward onto the bridle.

What to Do if...?

My horse won't come back from the extended trot.

Build an extra volte in at the corner. Ride the volte to calm the horse until he is once again accepting your aids.

My horse gets crooked while crossing the diagonal.

Practice simply riding a straight diagonal, without extending your trot.

My horse breaks into a canter.

Riding your horse correctly on the bridle and working on the rail, practice increasing your tempo a little at a time.

7.4 Changing Tempo

What Do I Need?

2 cones, 6 ground poles.

Setting Up

Position a cone at both D and G, 3–5 feet (1–1.5 m) from the rail, position the six ground poles so that they frame the line you are going to ride (see diagram).

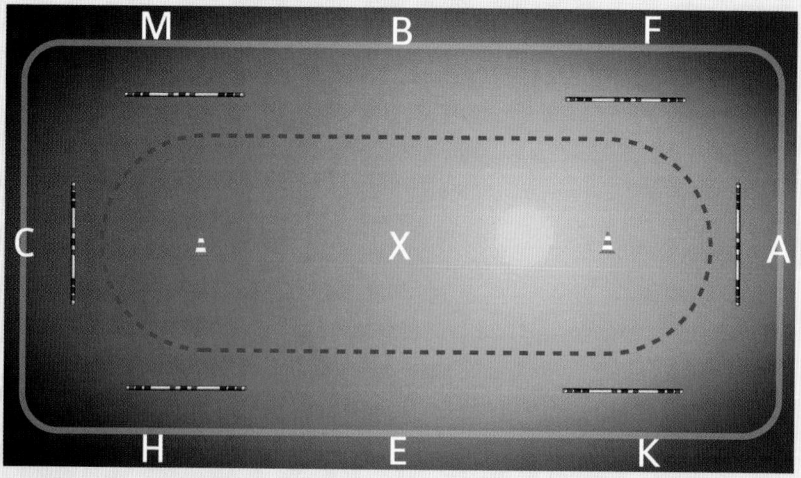

How Does This Exercise Work?

(1) Ride along the delineated line 4–6 feet (1.2–1.8 m) from the rail at, let's say, the trot. On the long sides, you can lengthen the trot stride.
(2) As soon as you are in line with the cone on the long side, use your weight aids to bring your horse back then ride half of a 15–20 meter circle around the cone (as opposed to riding deep corners). The ground poles set the boundary for your circle and prevent the horse from falling to the outside. As soon as you have finished your turn around the cone, breathe into your chest in order to lift your breastbone and, thereby, heighten engagement and tone. Drive your horse forward, more onto the bit, and allow his frame to expand.

Tip: Post the trot!

Aids: On the long sides, you should drive the horse forward more by using both legs and sending him onto the bit. Allow your hips to swing forward in order to increase the tempo. As soon as you approach the point where the turn begins, change the swing of your hips to be more upward ("your belt buckle should reach the ceiling!") and breathe into your chest. So, you should have the feeling that your breastbone is attached to a cord that is pulling upward. Make sure you don't develop a hollow back, which will block your hips from following.

What Is the Horse Learning?

To change his tempo in response to more refined aids.

Build engagement and tone by lifting through your breastbone as you inhale.

What Is the Rider Learning?

To keep the horse on the aids at the extended trot without the support of the rail. To bring the horse back through the corners using more refined weight aids.

What to Do if...?

My horse deviates from the designated line of travel and weaves down the long sides.

First, take away the change in tempo and just ride along on the designated line 4–6 feet (1.2–1.8 m) from the rail. Make sure that you sit straight in the saddle and frame your horse evenly with your aids on both sides.

My horse does not slow down in response to my weight aids and body energy.

Revisit and practice chapter 2.

7.5 Stop Sign

In this exercise, the hindquarters are activated, the shoulders are lifted, the hindquarters are lowered, and the horse's willing cooperation is encouraged.

What Do I Need?

Up to 6 cones.

Setting Up

This exercise offers many possible variations: a square—four cones spaced at least 32 feet (10 m) apart; a triangle—three cones positioned as a triangle and spaced at least 32 feet (10 m) apart; a hexagon (see diagram).

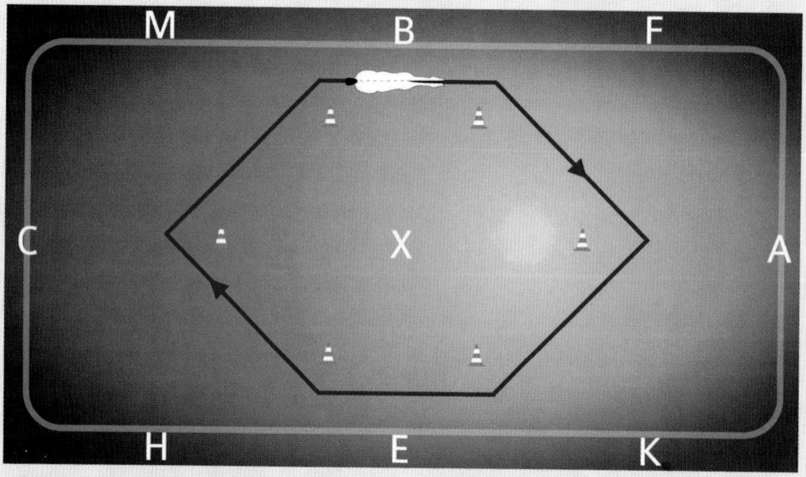

How Does This Exercise Work?

(1) Ride along the outside of the cones. Always maintain a consistent distance from the cones. On the straight lines, frame the horse according to your riding style.
(2) Western riders execute a quarter turn-on-the-haunches at each cone, while dressage riders execute a few steps of half-pass (see *Exercise 9.7*).

> **Tip:** In the turns, the horse must shift more weight onto his haunches and allow his shoulder to move freely through the corners. The horse must clearly step up beneath the center of gravity. In trot/canter, the tempo should be scaled back noticeably.

Aids: (Note: Classical dressage riders can find a description of the aids in Exercise 9.7.) The exercise can, of course, be ridden at the walk or trot.

When going straight, evenly distribute the weight aids, evenly apply leg aids, evenly guide with the reins (your shoulders are parallel).

When turning on the haunches, as soon as the horse's croup is even with the cone, your outside leg sends the horse's shoulder around. Your weight comes to the inside, the horse is positioned to the inside, and the outside rein lies against the neck. The inside leg becomes active only when the horse begins to fall onto his inside shoulder through the turn, or even positions himself toward the outside.

For a slight half-pass, your seat is lightly weighted to the inside, your inside leg drives the horse, while your outside leg is applied lightly in a guarding position. The outside rein regulates the horse while the inside rein positions him.

Ground poles also make a great visual barrier when used to mark the straight lines.

Heads Up! With difficult breeds or in some different riding styles, the outside leg can also come back while driving the horse forward, which supports the outside hind.

What Is the Horse Learning?

To lift through his shoulder and step up actively with his hind legs. To shift weight onto his hindquarters and respond to his rider's refined aids.

What Is the Rider Learning?

Feel and correct timing of the aids. To plan ahead and put the horse back onto his hindquarters.

What to Do if...?

My horse positions himself to the outside.

The horse is finding it difficult to maintain longitudinal bend through the turns and is leaning on his inside shoulder. Make your turn bigger and make sure that your inside leg is active and your inside rein positions the horse.

My horse doesn't turn but gets quick instead.

Review the acceptance of the leg aids with your horse (see ch. 2 *The Rein Aids*).

8. Straightness

The goal of this training exercise is for the horse to achieve Straightness through gymnastic exercises (Step 5 on Classical and Western Training Scales).

On both straight and bending lines, the horse should maintain balance, moving with his forehand and hindquarters aligned on the track he is being ridden. To make it happen, the horse's naturally occurring asymmetry must be brought into balance. Exercises that include lateral movements are extremely helpful here.

Lateral Movements (Shoulder-In, Shoulder-Out, Haunches-In, Haunches-Out, Half-Pass):
By lateral movements, one is referring to specific, learned movements that require the horse to move forward and sideways simultaneously. Lateral movements can be ridden at all gaits and through all ring figures. Lateral movements promote willing cooperation, balance, and smooth movement.

A distinction is made between lateral movements that are performed with the horse "bent in the direction of travel" (haunches-in, haunches-out, and half-pass) and with the horse "bent away from the direction of travel" (shoulder-in and shoulder-out).

For *shoulder-in* (forehand toward the center of the arena) and shoulder-out (forehand toward the rail), the bending horse travels on a straight line. Based on your riding style, the movement may be ridden on three or four tracks, respectively.

Haunches-in (also known as travers) and haunches-out (also known as renvers) are distinguished from one another only based on whether the haunches are positioned toward or away from the arena rail. For the horse, they constitute the same movement. He must maintain bend while moving along a straight line. Here too, your riding style will determine whether the horse is ridden on three or four tracks while executing this movement.

The *half-pass* is a laterally executed ring figure. It begins with shoulder-in, then becomes a half-pass across the diagonal, continuing as haunches-out when the horse arrives at the rail; the movement concludes with the horse being repositioned with shoulder-in in the new direction. In advanced training, the lateral movements can also be executed on a circle, a square, and a volte. Lateral movements on the smallest volte are referred to as the pirouette (ridden in haunches-in) or as the pirouette-in-haunches-out, respectively.

Note: In all lateral movements, the forehand must stay just slightly ahead of the hindquarters. Otherwise, the horse will lose rhythm, impulsion, and carrying ability.

Shoulder-In: The shoulder-in is a lateral movement in which the horse is bent away from the direction of travel. The haunches remain on the track while the forehand is guided toward the inside of the arena, until the inside hind leg is in line with the step of the outside foreleg. Depending on your riding style, the desired result is that the horse will be moving simultaneously on either three or four tracks.

For shoulder-in, the inside hind leg must lower

and bear more weight, which encourages the outside back muscles to stretch and the poll to loosen. In classical riding, the horse can stretch more deeply into the outside rein, resulting in a lighter contact on this rein. Shoulder-in requires the horse's forehand to shift and for the forehand to become attuned to the hindquarters, making this an especially important exercise for straightness.

In the beginning, only ride the horse at shoulder-in for a few moments to avoid overwhelming him. Instead of riding an entire long side in shoulder-in, only ask for a few strides. At the walk, shoulder-in can help horses to relax and balance. They will loosen up and stretch through the topline.

Aids: Weight your inside seat bone, allowing the horse to track up under his center of gravity with

his inside hind leg. Imagine you would like to begin riding a volte. Apply your inside leg at the girth to encourage your horse to bend. The inside rein positions the horse while the outside rein limits and lifts his outside shoulder. The rider's outside leg hangs in the guarding position.

The haunches lower and flex more pronouncedly during shoulder-in and the carrying ability of his hindquarters will improve.

How does shoulder-in influence the horse?

- Shoulder-in improves the basic gaits and the straightness of canter departs. Shoulder-in can also improve problems with rhythm at the trot.
- Shoulder-in supports a supple poll and relaxed jaw, releasing tension, and, thereby, perpetuating mental and physical relaxation.
- The stretch toward and connection with the outside rein are improved through shoulder-in.
- Shoulder-in at the trot activates the hindquarters, thereby helping with changes in tempo and the development of impulsion.
- Shoulder-in supports straightness and helps to even out asymmetry.
- Shoulder-in helps the horse to develop more carrying ability. It improves the piaffe and thereby, collection.

Half-Pass: The half-pass is a forward-sideways movement in trot or canter. It's similar to haunches-in, but here the horse is ridden on a diagonal line, parallel to the long side of the arena. The horse is positioned and bent in the direction of travel and his outside legs cross in front of his inside fore and hind legs as he executes this movement. If the horse's croup gets ahead of his shoulders in this movement, it compromises the carrying ability of his hindquarters. In this case, the horse is no longer stepping up under his center of gravity correctly.

If the horse's neck is bent too much in the direction of travel, he'll lean onto his inside shoulder. He'll be heavy in the hands and because he's falling onto his shoulder, forward movement will cease. In half-pass, the forehand always takes the lead.

Aids: The rider sits more on the inside seat bone in order to encourage the horse to bend and also to avoid burdening the stretched muscles along the outside topline. The inside leg drives at the girth and is responsible for maintaining the lateral bend. The outside leg lies a little behind the girth and, at the moment of departure, encourages the outside hind to step up under the center of gravity. The inside rein positions the horse while the outside rein limits the shoulder. Here, too, the rider's shoulders stay parallel to the horse's shoulders; the rider's hips, parallel to the horse's hips. It's easiest to initiate half-pass from shoulder-in or from a bending line.

How does half-pass influence the horse?

- Half-pass improves flying changes and encourages an uphill canter.
- Half-pass improves balance and enhances control over the horse's shoulders.
- Half-pass supports straightness and helps to even out asymmetries.
- Half-pass helps the horse to develop more carrying ability behind and improves collection.

Haunches-In and Haunches-Out: Along with the shoulder-in, haunches-in and haunches-out are among the most important exercises for straightening your horse.

Haunches-In is referred to as a forward-sideways movement during which the horse is slightly bent and maintaining a constant angle of approximately 30 degrees. He should move on three or four tracks.

The counter exercise to haunches-in is haunches-out. In haunches-in, the hindquarters are placed toward the inside of the arena and the forehand remains on the rail. The horse crosses both his forelegs and hind legs, while remaining lightly flexed to the inside. Haunches-in can be ridden on both straight and bending lines. In haunches-out, the hindquarters remain on the rail as the forehand is placed to the inside. As this takes place, the horse is still bent in the direction of travel, as in haunches-in.

In each case, the goal is to teach the horse to step toward the center of gravity with his outside hind, and by doing so, carry more weight on that leg. Haunches-in and haunches-out both work to lighten and lift the inside shoulder as the outside hind leg takes on more weight, and the horse loads and flexes his haunches more.

Heads Up! The horse's croup must never get ahead! The shoulder remains the leader in order to ensure correct weight bearing.

In Western riding, the croup is often driven toward the inside and room is made for the shoulder by the rider "stretching" her inside leg out of the way. The weight is also often to the outside—the horse is sent away from the weight. This method of driving the croup to the inside leads to muscular flexibility and lends itself to an easier canter departure. However, it does not lead to a shoulder that is correctly aligned with the forehand, as, in this instance, the shoulder has not been driven into place by the rider's inside leg. Nevertheless, this remains a very effective approach for Western riding.

Aids: The rider sits more on the inside seat bone in order to foster the horse's bend, and to avoid added burden to the stretched muscles along his outside topline. The inside leg is applied at the girth and is responsible for maintaining lateral bend, while the outside leg hangs a little behind the girth and, at the moment of departure, asks the outside hind leg to step up under the horse's center of gravity. The rider's center of gravity—as if by instinct—should shift forward and to the inside, in the direction of the horse's inside shoulder. The inside rein positions the horse and the outside rein limits the shoulder. And, as with the shoulder-in, the rider's shoulders remain parallel to the horse's shoulders and the rider's hips remain parallel to the horse's hips.

8.1 Counter-Canter

This exercise is useful for improving canter on the true lead or for developing the counter-canter. In the beginning with a young or unbalanced horse, you only want to school the true canter lead and avoid asking the horse to depart into canter on the outside lead. Later, the horse should become equally comfortable departing into the true canter or the counter-canter. In true canter, the horse initiates the canter from his outside hind leg, followed by the inside hind and outside foreleg moving together as a diagonal pair, then finally by the inside foreleg, which is immediately followed by a moment of suspension. In counter-canter, the exact opposite takes place (beginning with the departure into canter from the inside hind). This means, as soon as we ride a canter on the left lead while we are tracking to the right (or the other way around) we are riding the counter-canter.

Setting Up

You can use ground poles to set a boundary line as you school this exercise.

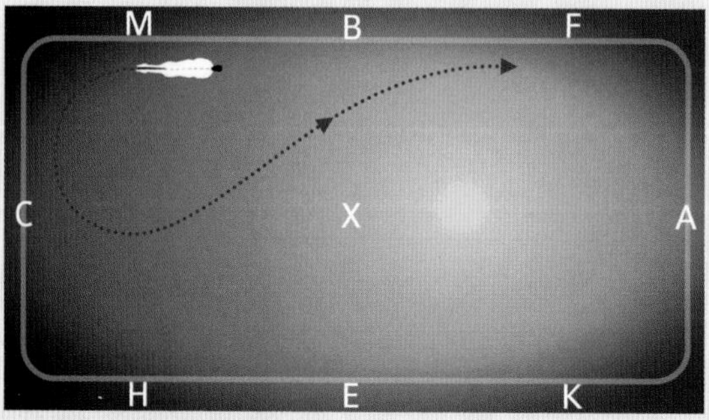

How Does This Exercise Work?

(1) Begin on the left lead canter, tracking left. Ride the whole arena, turning as you come out of a corner halfway across the short side. Stay in left lead canter until you reach E or B, respectively.

(2) Praise your horse if he maintains his left lead canter. In the beginning, it can be helpful to position him to the outside (counter-flexion), though later on you want the horse to be straight during this exercise.

Tip: Use your aids to frame your horse as if, with each canter stride, you are asking him for a brand new departure into canter.

What to Do if...?

My horse breaks to the trot.

Maintain positive body engagement and ride "through" at the canter. The most likely scenario is that your horse lacks muscular strength. Only ride the counter-canter for a little bit at a time and build it up gradually over many days and weeks.

My horse changes lead.

Transition your horse down to the walk and ask again for the canter on the desired lead.

As soon as I straighten my horse, he switches his lead.

Be gentle as you position your horse. Make sure that your horse is already responding well to your weight and leg aids in the true canter. If the true canter is being ridden with lots of positioning and rein aids, it is common that the horse will interpret the re-positioning as a request for a flying change.

8.2 On the Inside Track

Most horses and riders remain on the rail as they school. Therefore, horses and people become dependent upon following the rail, and the outside aids do not really come into play as much as they should. The horses are just sticking to the rail.

How Does This Exercise Work?

Ride this exercise on the inside track, 3–4 feet (1–1.3 m) off the rail, initially using the whole arena. Later, you can incorporate ring figures for variety. Frame the horse with your aids.

> **Tip:** Look ahead and take note of the distance to the rail. The goal is to maintain the same distance to the rail whether you are riding straight or bending lines without the horse wavering toward the inside or outside.

What Is the Horse Learning?

To be ridden without dependence on the rail.

What Is the Rider Learning?

To correctly frame the horse.

What to Do if...?

My horse pushes through his outside shoulder.

Ride along the inside track. Frame your horse with your aids. The instant you notice your horse beginning to drift toward the rail with his shoulder, position him to the outside. Ride in counter-flexion until your horse lifts through that shoulder and comes onto the aids with willing cooperation. Then position your horse to the inside and continue.

Mistakes that can occur during counter positioning:

My horse is flexing to the outside, but he is also moving toward the outside.

Review *Exercise 3.4*.

My horse tilts at the poll and refuses to come through on the aids.

Make sure you are riding with a yielding hand (taking rein, giving rein). Hold your inside hand a bit higher (remember, if you're tracking left, the right rein becomes the inside hand in counter-flexion!) and take your other hand slightly to the side.

8.3 Combining Lateral Movements

With this exercise, you'll coordinate the lateral movements. The horse learns to step sideways up under his center of gravity and to activate his hindquarters. The exercise lends itself to improving the half-pass.

What Do I Need?

1 cone.

Setting Up

Position the cone in a corner of the riding arena, so that you can comfortably ride a volte around the cone.

How Does This Exercise Work?

(1) Ride the whole arena at a collected trot or jog. On the long side approaching the cone, begin to ride shoulder-in.
(2) Before the corner, "melt" out of shoulder-in and begin riding a large volte around the cone.
(3) When you are about halfway around the volte, transition to riding a half-pass back toward the rail. Maintain the flexion from the volte while driving the horse forward and sideways. Trot around the whole arena (posting).

Tip: The transition into half-pass will flow best when you make sure the horse takes his first step sideways with his inside front leg.

What Is the Horse Learning?

Relaxation and throughness. Strengthening of the hindquarters.

What Is the Rider Learning?

Coordination of the various transition aids. Riding half-pass.

What to Do if...?

My horse will not go from the volte into the half-pass.

> Give a clear cue for sideward movement from the outside, guarding leg. Be timely in giving that leg aid. Look in the direction of the movement. It can also be helpful to "point the way" with your inside rein.

My horse does not get back to the rail.

> Set up the half-pass at a steeper angle. Contain the forward movement with the outside rein and give the horse clear aids to move laterally. It could be that the horse does not yet have enough strength to step sideways under his center of gravity this pronouncedly. Practice diverse lateral movements to build up your horse's strength.

My horse's haunches get ahead of his forehand.

> Look in the direction of travel. Make sure you are not inadvertently pulling your outside rein too far back. Guide your horse by opening your inside rein. To check whether the forehand is truly leading, transition out of the half-pass and back into shoulder-in.

8.4 Bending and Straight Lines

With this exercise, you school the change between bending and straight lines. Here, you can check the horse's rhythm and balance. Trotting over the ground poles loosens the horse's shoulders and strengthens the hindquarters.

What Do I Need?

6 cones, 3 ground poles.

Setting Up

Set up the ground poles for trotting about 4 feet (1.3 m) apart along the centerline between A and X (see diagram). Four of the cones should stand to the right and left of the ends of the ground poles, in between them. The other two cones should be positioned by C, so that you can ride a volte around each of them.

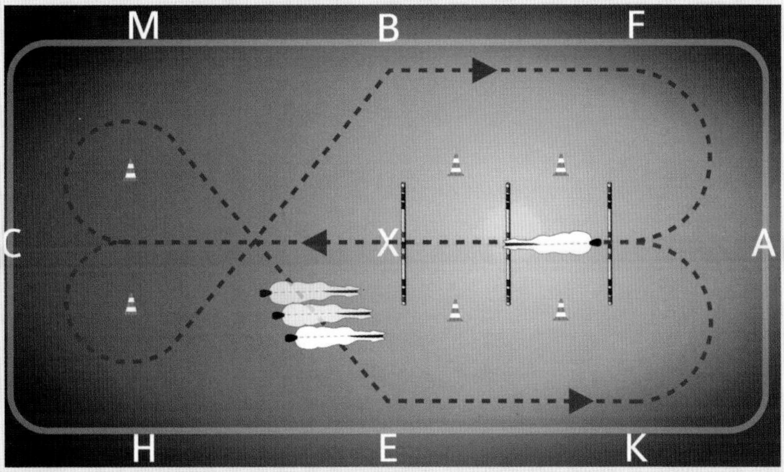

How Does This Exercise Work?

(1) Using the whole arena, ride at the sitting trot. At A, turn up the centerline. Ride through the passageway of poles/cones. Continue up the centerline.
(2) Take the horse back at the trot and ride a volte around a cone. After completing half of the volte, begin a half-pass toward the rail. When you reach the rail at B (or E respectively), position the horse straight ahead.
(3) Repeat the exercise, this time riding a volte around the other cone. Build in breaks where you ride around the entire arena at the posting trot.

Aids: To move the horse toward E in a half-pass, position and bend the horse to the right, in the direction of the movement. Carry the positioning over from the volte. Shift your weight to the right. Apply your right leg at the girth. The left leg lies in a guarding position on the horse's side. With your left leg, give a clear aid to the horse that he should cross his legs. When you reach the rail, reposition the horse straight ahead. Apply the opposite aids to ride the half-pass to the left.

What Is the Horse Learning?

The horse is learning to maintain an even rhythm at the trot and obedience to the leg aids. He'll stay freer through his shoulder and strengthen his hindquarters. →

What Is the Rider Learning?

The difference between bending and straight lines. Refinement of the aids. Precise control over the lines.

What to Do if...?

My horse does not move straight ahead after the half-pass.

Check your aids. If your aids are correct, take a break, ride the whole arena on a long rein then try it again.

My horse wavers along the centerline.

Frame the horse evenly on both sides with your rein and leg aids. Distribute your weight evenly. Don't fold at the hip, and stay loose as you swing with the horse's movement. To improve balance, school straight lines without relying on the rail or other marked boundaries.

My half-pass becomes too shallow.

Regulate the horse with your outside rein. Shift your weight in the direction of travel, push with your pelvis and look in the direction that you want to go. Allow your outside leg to lie farther back and give the horse a clear lateral cue. If necessary, use a dressage whip to tap the horse's croup on the outside.

Half-pass: the rider's shoulders are parallel to horse's shoulders; rider's hips are parallel to horse's hips.

8.5 Schooling the Circle with Haunches-Out

Haunches-in and haunches-out train flexion and bend, but also loosen and lift the shoulder. Rideability and willing cooperation are encouraged along with coordination and correct understanding of the rider's various aids.

What Do I Need?

1 cone, 4 ground poles.

Setting Up

Position the cone in the center of the circle and use the poles to form a "cross" around the cones (see diagram).

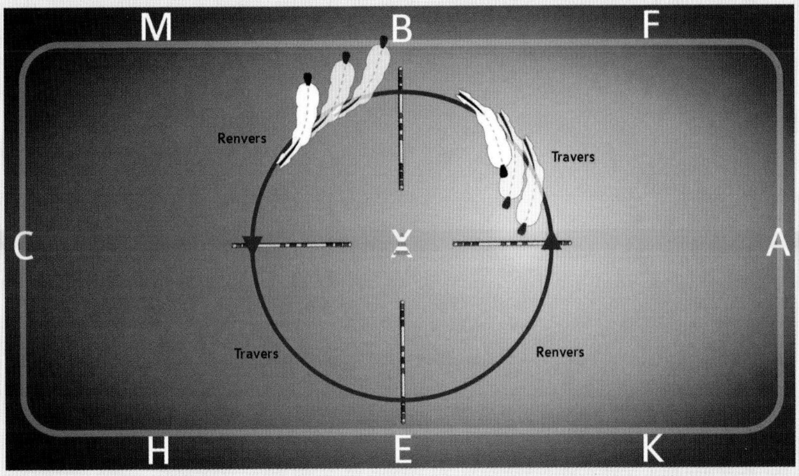

How Does This Exercise Work?

(1) Begin by riding this exercise at the walk (later, in other gaits). Riding a few feet from the rail, come onto the circle.

(2) As you ride each quarter-circle, switch between haunches-in and haunches-out. As you transition between these two movements, position the horse straight ahead and cross over the ground pole. This exercise can also be ridden without the ground pole.

What Is the Horse Learning?

Flexion and bend. To loosen up and lift through his shoulder. To correctly understand the rider's aids. To cross with his legs and activate the haunches.

What Is the Rider Learning?

Coordination and application of the various aids. To divide and thereby organize the circle.

What to Do if...?

My horse hesitates in the transition from haunches-in to haunches-out.

Take a step back. School both the haunches-in and haunches-out individually. When you next try this exercise, do a complete circle in haunches-in before transitioning to haunches-out and vice versa. Gradually, shorten the time in between the transition. In between the transition from haunches-in to haunches-out (and vice versa) be sure to position the horse straight ahead.

8.6 Haunches-In on the Half-Circle

This exercise increases your horse's willing cooperation and rideability. It can improve the way of going at walk, trot, and canter and can help with the development of canter pirouettes.

What Do I Need?

1 cone.

Setting Up

Position the cone in any corner of the arena. The cone is the center point of your half-circle to change direction.

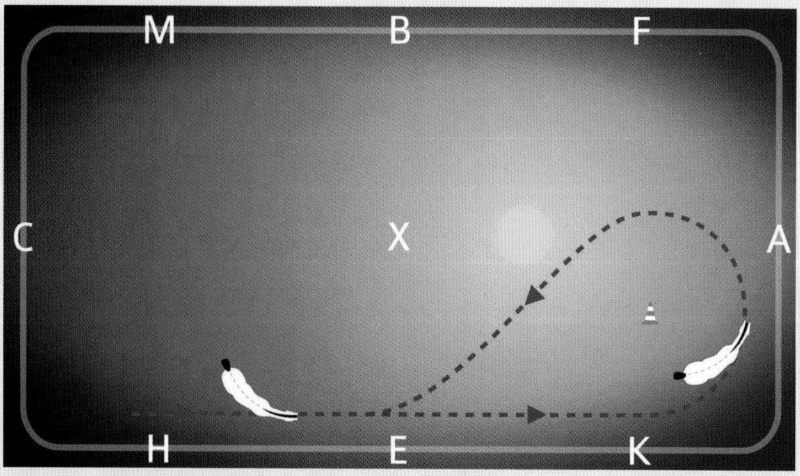

How Does This Exercise Work?

(1) Ride the entire long side of the arena in haunches-in. Near the cone in the corner, continue in haunches-in, but begin riding a half-volte to change direction.

(2) Once you have returned to the rail in your new direction, straighten the horse. Depending on the level of education and training, you can potentially add in a transition here, either to a higher gait or to an extension within your current gait. (The haunches-in is explained in detail on p. 102.)

What Is the Horse Learning?

To pay attention to the rider's aids. Willing cooperation and rideability. Activation of the hindquarters. This exercise hones gracefulness and balance for lateral movements and in transitions. Improvement of the gaits. Lowering the hindquarters for the upward transition to canter. A precursor to canter pirouettes.

What Is the Rider Learning?

To coordinate diverse aids. Preparation for riding canter pirouettes.

What to Do if...?

As my horse executes the half-circle to change direction, he falls out of haunches-in.

The hindquarters must step up actively and the forehand must lift. Begin by training the haunches-in on a circle, gradually making it smaller. It can take several weeks for the musculature to build adequately. Then try the exercise again.

My horse veers heavily off the half-circle.

More than others, heavy horses tend to fall onto the shoulders when the hindquarters are not truly active. With targeted training, work to strengthen the hindquarters. For example, using the whole arena, ride four strides of haunches-in then transition to a very active trot. Repeat this exercise multiple times then try again to reverse direction on the half-circle while riding in haunches-in.

Variation: Ride this exercise with haunches-in at the canter and also ride haunches-in at the counter-canter. This is the introduction to canter pirouettes. To conclude, you can continue in counter-canter, execute a simple change of lead, or transition downward to the trot.

8.7 Flying Changes

The flying change is a very elegant way of going from one canter lead to the other. Horses happily execute flying changes without a rider when they are loose in the pasture. In any case, however, it is not that easy for a horse to do a flying change beneath a rider, as it requires much balance and coordination on the part of the horse—and a rider who has good balance and a feel for timing.

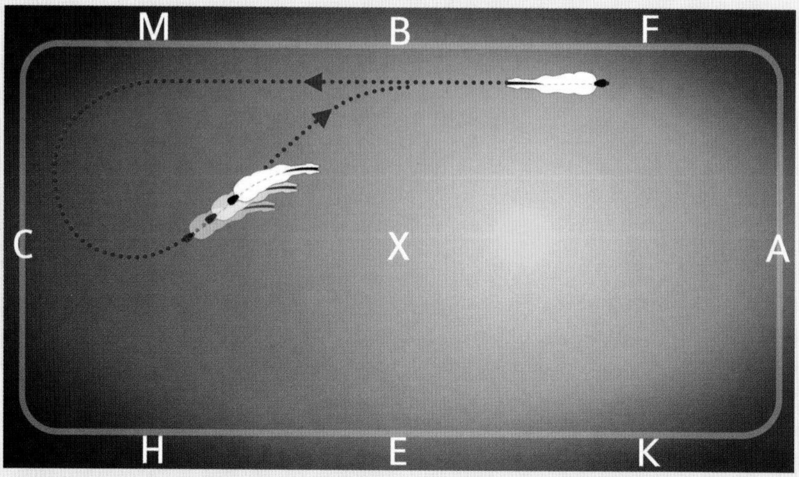

How Does This Exercise Work?

(1) Tracking left and riding left-lead canter, come out of the corner and ride a half-circle to change direction. Move your horse away from the centerline and toward the rail at B (or E, respectively). The horse can be positioned toward the middle of the arena.

(2) As soon as you reach the point of contact with the rail, shift your weight to the inside (pushing your inside hip forward) and apply your leg aid. The positioning of the horse does not change. Ride on in right-lead canter. The aids take place simultaneously.

Note: You can also ride the half-circle out of the corner in half-pass. Doing so means that when you reach the point of contact with the rail, you must not only shift your weight and change your leg position but also reposition the horse in the new direction of travel.

Tip: Ride the movement all the way to the rail.

Aids: If you're beginning in left-lead canter, then your weight must be left, the left leg drives at the girth (or a hand-width behind) and the outside leg lies in a guarding position a bit behind the girth. At first, the horse is flexed to the left, then this changes to the right as he moves back toward the rail. At this point, the right rein does the positioning and the left rein is in a regulating position. Upon arriving at the rail, the right leg shifts forward, the left moves back, and the weight shifts to the right.

We speak of a flying change when the horse executes a change of lead during the moment of suspension at the canter.

Tip: Stay calm and practice patience as you school flying changes. Praise your horse the instant he changes his lead.

Tip: Count along with the canter strides every time that your hips swing forward. Begin to do so four canter strides before you reach the rail: "3, 2, 1, *hop*." At "hop," shift your aids and allow the horse to change.

What Is the Horse Learning?

To free up his shoulder, which makes the flying change possible.

What Is the Rider Learning?

To pay close attention to her aids and to apply them simultaneously.

What to Do if...?

My horse just runs on in counter-canter.

Calm your horse, transition downward, and pick up the true canter in your new direction. After a couple of strides, transition downward again, change direction, and retry the exercise.

As another alternative, you might place a ground pole at the end of the long side, before the corner. Horses can have an easier time changing lead over the pole because of the longer moment of suspension.

My horse changes lead up front, but not behind.

In chapter 9, you will find further exercises that can help your horse learn to change his lead correctly – from back to front.

9. Collection or Total Willing Cooperation

The sixth point on the Training Scales is: Collection/Total Willing Cooperation (Classical) and Complete Willing Cooperation/Natural Self-Carriage (Western).

We speak of collection when the horse takes more weight onto his hindquarters, clearly lowering and flexing his haunches, while moving with straightness and impulsion. The forehand lifts and you are able to recognize a clear uphill tendency. The horse's movement appears lighter and effortless; the horse becomes more and more willingly cooperative.

Collection serves to develop and improve the horse's balance and, by doing so, it fosters self-carriage. Every horse, no matter what the riding style, needs carrying power in the hindquarters and an elastic, lifted, loosely swinging back.

Why do we speak of "complete willing cooperation" and not of "collection" in Western riding? In Western riding, horses are certainly also collected, just not in the classical style. Because in Western riding the goal is a willingly cooperative and obedient horse, rather than movements such as the canter pirouette or passage, we speak of "total willing cooperation" for the Western horse.

In classical riding, collection is established through suspension between the driving aids and the connection with the bit. The horse lifts his forehand and his poll (between the 1st and 2nd vertebrae) becomes his highest point. The hindquarters lower and the pelvis tilts as a result of deep flexion in the haunches. Furthermore, the bridge of the horse's nose stays just ahead of the vertical. The underside of the neck and the poll remain relaxed.

Heads Up! The raising of the forehand is the result of flexion in the haunches. The more pronouncedly the horse lowers his hindquarters, the higher he will lift through his neck. In collection, the horse raises himself. The lifting of the forehand may not ever be forced by the rider's hands. Through the lowering and flexing of the haunches, the horse's center of gravity shifts, freeing up the forehand. His stride will become more elevated. The horse demonstrates the uphill tendency.

Heads Up! A correctly ridden horse lifts the forehand in a way that is related to what is happening with the hindquarters. False lifting of the forehand is forced by the rider's hand and the horse's hips are not lowered.

9.1 Riding Corners

Riding corners correctly is not just important for dressage tests. Doing so also helps your horse to step clearly under the center of gravity and by doing so, to carry more weight on his hindquarters.

What Do I Need?

1–4 cones and/or 2–8 ground poles.

Setting Up

Position several cones in the corners about 16 feet (5 m) from the long side and 16 feet from the short side.

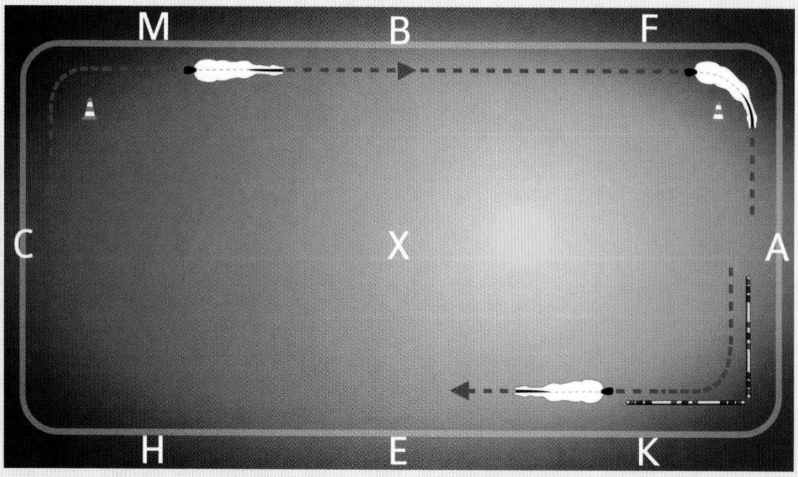

How Does This Exercise Work?

(1) Traveling on the track near the rail, ride deep into the corner. Frame your horse with your aids and stabilize his hindquarters.

Aids: Drive the horse clearly into the corner/turn with the inside leg, so that the inside hind leg tracks up under the center of gravity. Frame your horse with the outside aids, to prevent him from evading. After the corner, continue in a diligent trot and begin again after the next corner (see also p. 130 for more on turning).

(2) If this all goes well, you can try the same exercise, this time riding about 3-4 feet (1–1.3 m) off the rail. Position two ground poles in the corner in an L-shape, which now constitute the corner of the arena. It's important to trot diligently forward after the turn, so that the horse continues to track up clearly under his center of gravity as he travels down the long side.

Tip: Look deliberately ahead into the corner. In order to avoid the horse cutting the corners, you can also occasionally allow him to stand quietly in the corner.

What Is the Horse Learning?

To develop more carrying ability and more noticeable bend.

What Is the Rider Learning?

To ride correctly into the corners and to allow her horse to step more definitively up under the center of gravity.

What to Do if...?

In the corners, my horse's hindquarters move to the outside.

The horse is evading to the outside and no longer stepping up under his center of gravity. Your horse is lacking in correct musculature. In this direction, practice haunches-in more often (see *Exercise 8.6*).

My horse falls to the inside.

Your horse is not actively stepping up under the center of gravity and he is heavy on the forehand. Practice riding shoulder-in (see *Exercise 8.3*).

9.2 Counter-Volte at the Canter

This exercise lends itself well to improving the canter and is preparation for a correct, back-to-front, complete and springy flying change.

What Do I Need?

2 cones.

Setting Up

The cones are positioned at least 32 feet (10 m) apart from one another, in the riding arena or in a field.

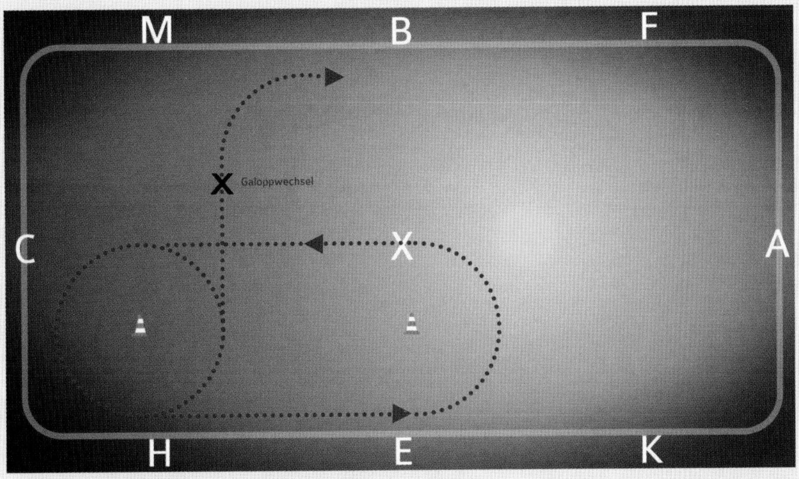

How Does This Exercise Work?

(1) Ride at a canter around both cones, making an oval shape.

(2) As soon as your horse falls onto his outside shoulder, begin to ride a volte in counter-flexion (see *Exercise 3.5*) around the next cone. As soon as he lifts that shoulder, return to riding the oval. In counter-flexion, what is now your inside leg (normally the outside in this direction) is applied at the girth, in order to lift the horse's shoulder. →

Tip: Think about your correct weight aids!

What to Do if…?

In one direction, my horse falls to the inside as opposed to the outside.

Only ride this exercise in the direction in which your horse falls to the outside and, therefore, in which it is also more difficult to execute a flying change of lead.

My horse breaks.

This exercise requires lots of muscular strength. Give your horse time and don't overdo it with this exercise.

This is also an exercise where a complete but short training session is better.

My horse braces against me as soon as I ride him in counter-flexion.

Make sure that you are riding this exercise first and foremost using your weight and leg aids.

9.3 Half-Circles

This exercise is a collected exercise at the trot. This is an important one for the dressage rider: collected trot. And for the Western rider: jog. Through the regular changes of direction, you can check whether the horse is moving straight and also school straightness further.

What Do I Need?

4 cones.

Setting Up

Position the cones along the centerline. There should be a distance of 26 feet (8 m) between the cones.

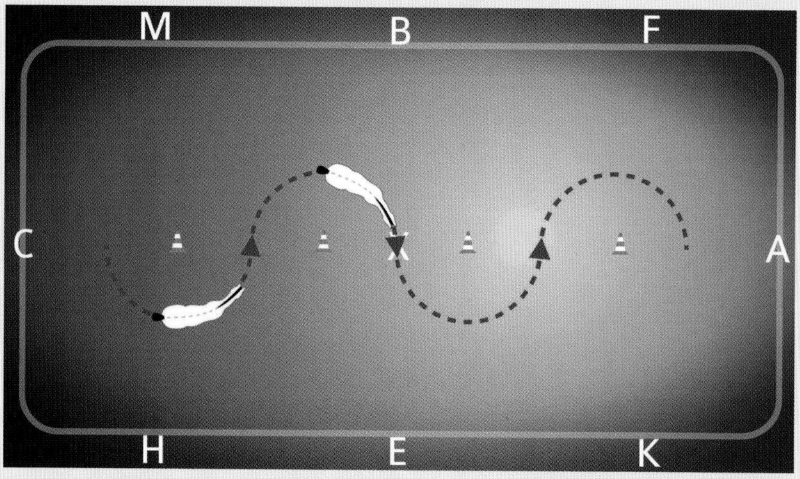

How Does This Exercise Work?

(1) Tracking left, ride a half-circle around the first cone, immediately followed by a half-circle to the right around the next cone. Continue with this pattern.
(2) Ride this exercise at the trot. Depending on the training level of your horse, this exercise can be difficult at first. The horse must first learn how to lower and shift weight onto his hindquarters in order to be able to execute a good turn around the cone.

Aids: In the volte, position the horse in the direction of travel with your inside leg and apply your inside leg aid. Use your outside rein and outside leg to limit the horse on the outside.

Tip: Always look ahead, directing your gaze in the direction of the arena wall or fence and not looking down at the cones or ground. As you change direction between the cones, ride the horse straight for a couple of strides and then carefully position him in the new direction. Test the results of the exercise by riding the long side at the trot and making sure you can maintain the collected trot.

What Is the Horse Learning?

To take more weight on his hindquarters. Tight turns at the trot. Flexibility with positioning and bend. To travel straight in between the turns. Willing cooperation. Consistent movement through the shoulders.

What Is the Rider Learning?

How to ride tight turns at the trot. Positioning and bending. To ride straight in between the turns. To collect the horse onto his hindquarters. Collected trot/jog.

→

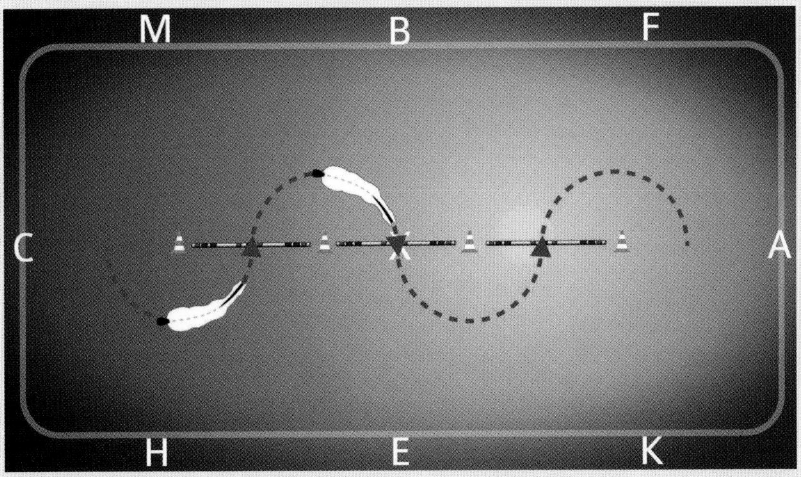

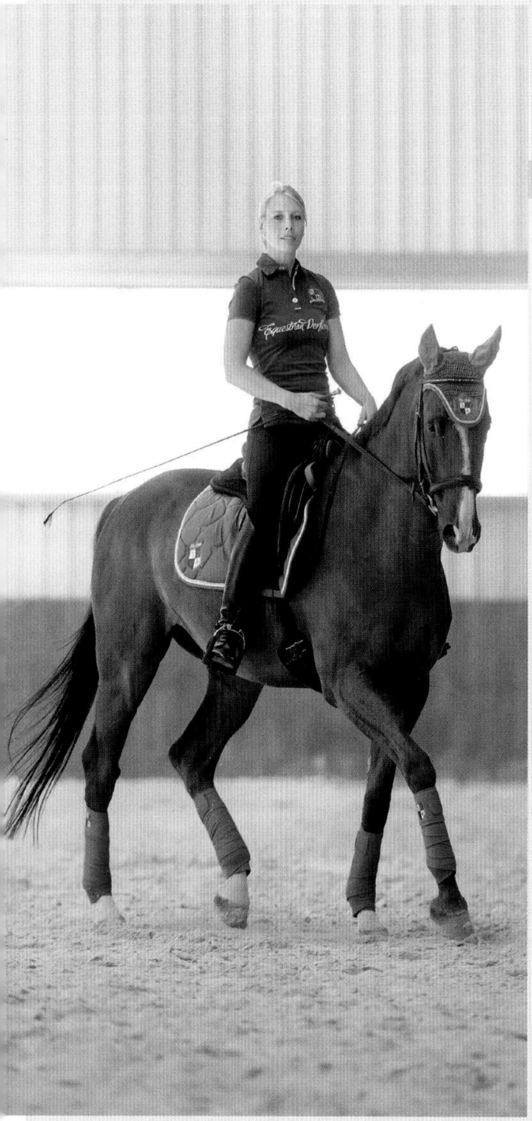

This exercise helps your horse develop noticeably more carrying ability.

Heads Up! The collected trot is possible only when the necessary muscles have been built up. Potentially, this can take many weeks to develop.

What to Do if...?

Over time, my horse gets slower.

Often, the horse does not become more collected, but instead gets lazier. Instead of carrying more weight on the hindquarters, the horse allows his hind end to trail. You are riding more with your rein aids than your leg aids. Try out the following variation.

Half-Circles: Variation

What Do I Need? 4 cones, 3 ground poles.

Setting Up: Set up the cones as described above on a long side (see diagram p. 119). Position a ground pole in between the cones.

How Does This Exercise Work?

Ride the exercise as described on p. 119. If the horse crosses over the poles without any problem, the hindquarters are tracking up well. The training was successful.

What to Do if...?

My horse does not travel smoothly.

Focus your attention just on the path of travel and not on the correct bending and positioning of the horse. Do the exercise a couple of times this way, then turn your attention to the challenges with positioning and bend.

My horse gets quicker and takes uneven strides.

Stop riding the exercise and instead ride the whole arena. Trot briskly forward (possibly in posting trot) until your horse is rhythmic once more.

My horse hits the ground poles with his front feet.

The horse is moving too heavily on his forehand. Go back to *Exercise 5.6* or *6.2.* Consider your horse's level of training. On larger turns, practice riding with straightness and having your horse step up actively from behind.

My horse hits the ground poles with his back feet.

The horse is not really stepping up under the center of gravity. Use *Exercise 4.4* in order to train the horse to track up actively and with straightness.

9.4 Half-Pass at Canter

In order to execute this movement, your horse must be truly on your aids. Shortening and lengthening the canter strides should already be a familiar exercise.

How Does This Exercise Work?

(1) Cantering on the right lead, turn down the centerline at A. Use your seat to shorten the canter and allow your horse to half-pass toward the right. Decide for yourself, how steep or how gradual you want the half-pass to be. Your goal should be just before M.
(2) Here, build in a change of lead. Now, ride on the left lead from H to K. At A, turn up the centerline again and this time half-pass to the left. Make sure to take lots of breaks.

Tip: Before riding the half-pass, it's vital to have your horse responding well to your seat and leg aids. Retract your horse step by step using your seat, without allowing too much pressure to build on the reins. Drive with your inside leg at the girth. The outside leg controls the sideways movement and cues the half-pass. The horse is always positioned in the direction of travel. Look ahead, sit to the inside.

Aids: While riding half-pass and preparing for the flying change, pay more attention to your hips. The right hip swings forward (moment of suspension). As you approach the rail, count the strides "3, 2, 1, hop" and with "hop," shift your hips so that your left hip now swings forward. Apply your leg aid and bring your inside shoulder a little forward. This should all happen at the same time (during the moment of suspension), so that the horse can easily change lead.

What Is the Horse Learning?

Obedience to the leg aids. Improved canter. Increased willing cooperation. To lengthen and shorten the canter stride. Tight turns. Flexibility with bending and positioning. Flying changes. Improved overall conditioning.

What Is the Rider Learning?

To influence the canter stride using her seat. Refinement of the aids. Riding tight turns at the canter. Orientation within the riding arena. Schooling of half-pass at the canter and flying changes.

→

→ 9.4 4 Half-Pass at Canter

As you initiate the half-pass, you should already be looking toward the point where you will complete the movement.

What to Do if...?

My horse does not shorten his canter stride.

Consider why this might be so: is it possible his musculature is not developed sufficiently for this exercise? Go back to schooling *Exercises 4.5* and *3.5* at canter, or *7.4* at canter.

Is your horse overwhelmed mentally?

Transition to the walk on a short rein, then ride quietly at all gaits until your horse is relaxed and supple once again.

9.5 Cone Game 2 (with Half-Pass)

This exercise lends itself to encouraging the horse to carry more weight on his hindquarters. With the half-pass and voltes in this exercise, you can train the horse to carry more weight behind and to activate his hindquarters. This exercise prepares the horse for collected movements and allows the horse to come more fully onto the aids.

What Do I Need?

3–4 cones.

Setting Up

See *Cone Game, Exercise 6.1.*

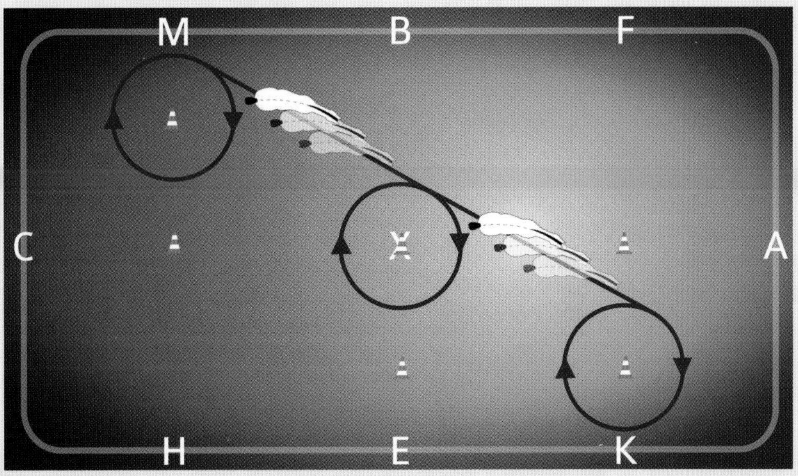

How Does This Exercise Work?

This exercise is divided into different levels of difficulty. One thing applies at every level: the horse always stays bent in one direction!

Ride a volte, let's say to the right, around one of the cones. Use the aids for half-pass to the right to move the horse to the next cone, where you can again ride a volte to the right around the cone.

(1) **Four Cones:** Ride a volte to the right around the cone at K (not depicted here). Half-pass to the right to the cone at X. Here, again ride a volte to the right. Then ride straight ahead to the next cone at G. Ride one-and-a-half voltes around the cone. Then, half-pass to the cone by E. There, ride a volte and then straight back to the cone by K, where you can begin the exercise all over again.

(2) **Three Cones:** Ride a volte to the right around the cone at M. Half-pass to the cone at X. At this cone, ride a volte to the right around the cone (see diagram) and then again ride the horse in a half-pass to the right to the cone at K. Here, ride one-and-a-half voltes and then ride the horse in a half-pass to the right back to the cone by M, where you began.

(3) Apply all of this in the opposite direction with a left-hand bend: H–X–F–X–H.

(4) Now you can get creative, finding your own trail through the "Cone Woods." But think about it: the horse must always stay bent in one direction! →

→ 9.5 Cone Game 2 (with Half-Pass)

For Experts: Flying changes are going well and the half-pass, too? Then you can ride this exercise with changes of direction. Half-pass in canter to the left, lead change, volte in canter to the right, and so on. This exercise improves the canter and flying changes.

Tip: Look ahead and plan your course ahead of time.

Aids: For the half-pass, put more weight on your inside seat bone and apply your inside leg at the girth, in order to achieve longitudinal bend and forward movement. The outside leg lies a bit farther back and drives the horse sideways, applied always when the outside hind leg pushes off. The inside rein positions the horse, and the outside rein limits him. The rider's shoulders are parallel to the horse's shoulders; the rider's hips parallel to the horse's hips.

What Is the Horse Learning?

To carry more weight on the hindquarters. To lower and flex his haunches and shorten his frame. Collection and willing cooperation.

What Is the Rider Learning?

Body engagement. A feel for the horse lowering and flexing his haunches. Spatial awareness.

What to Do if...?

On the volte after the half-pass, my horse falls onto his inside shoulder.

> Bring the engagement of the half-pass with you into the volte and drive the horse forward more, in order to activate the inside hind leg. Make sure that the shoulder is leading in half-pass and that you are only using your inside rein to position the horse, not to pull on him. You could switch it up between shoulder-in and half-pass, in order to ensure the horse is lifting through that shoulder.

The addition of a volte in counter-flexion after the half-pass can help to lift the shoulder in Western riding. For example, after a half-pass to the right, begin a volte around the next cone. As soon as the horse falls onto his inside shoulder, bend to the left in a counter-volte. Afterward, continue to ride along the planned course.

9.6 Shoulder Control

In this exercise, you lift your horse's shoulders, ride him straight, and improve willing cooperation. Correct flying changes will get lighter and more harmonious through this exercise. Prerequisites are the flying change, counter-canter and a horse that is willingly cooperative at true canter.

What Do I Need?

Cones.

Setting Up

Position some cones (for example, use 5) in a row, with a minimum distance of 50 feet (15 m) in between.

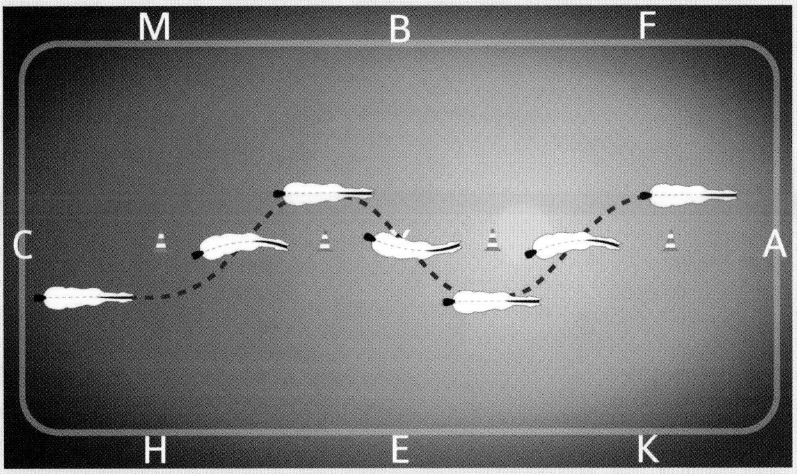

How Does This Exercise Work?

(1) To begin with, ride straight ahead, along the outside of the row of cones, but very near to the row.

(2) At the second cone, position your horse to the outside (in counter-flexion) and send your horse's shoulders to the inside (see Exercise 2.1). Now continue to ride along the inside of the row of cones.

(3) This time, ride along the outside of the row of cones. At the second cone, position your horse to the outside and move him to the inside. Along the row of cones, ride a flying change of lead and then ride to the inside of the row of cones in counter-canter.

(4) Now, ride along the outside of the row of cones. At the second cone, position your horse to the outside and drive him to the inside. Along the row of the cones, ride a flying change of lead, continuing to travel along the row of cones, passing one cone. When you reach the following cone, keep your horse positioned to the inside, driving him to the outside of the row. When you arrive along the row of cones, change your lead back to true canter and canter along past the last cone on the outside.

(5) Finally, you can gradually increase the difficulty of the exercise until you are moving your horse sideways and allowing a flying change at every cone.

Tip: Also ride this exercise once through in true canter, without having your horse do a flying change at all.

→

Aids: In this exercise, the various aids from counter-flexion, shifting of the forehand, and flying changes come together.

What Is the Horse Learning?

To lift his shoulder and to wait for the rider's aids. Encourages both the willing cooperation of the horse and the flying change.

What Is the Rider Learning?

To prepare the horse for the flying change, as she would later when performing a flying change on a straightway.

Note: This exercise lends itself to preparation for riding a flying change on the straightway. Together with Exercise 5.2 ridden at canter, this exercise is the perfect preparation for Western riders. For dressage riders, too, this is a good exercise for riding multiple flying changes in succession.

What to Do if...?

My horse still changes lead up front before he changes behind.

Within this exercise, build in *Exercise 9.2*, in order to more definitively lift the horse's shoulder.

9.7 Canter Pirouette

This exercise improves the horse's ability to carry weight on the hindquarters and to lower and flex the haunches. The horse collects himself at canter and becomes more powerful behind. The ability of the inside hind to take more of the load improves and the canter clearly has more uphill tendency.

What Do I Need?

4 cones.

Setting Up

For this exercise, all cones should have a distance of at least 32 feet (10 m) in between.

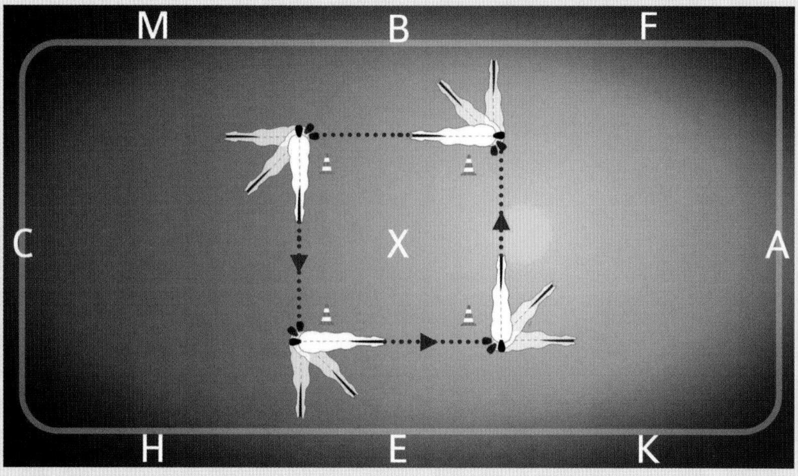

→ 9.7 Canter Pirouette

How Does This Exercise Work?

(1) Practice 90-degree turns with your horse at the canter: Ride a square to the outside of the cones.
(2) At the cone, turn your horse 90 degrees in an easy half-pass, which will require two or three canter strides.

Aids: On the straightway, ride your horse in a collected canter. When you arrive at the cone, sit to the inside and use your inside leg to bend your horse. The outside leg limits him and also has the task of supporting his outside hind leg. The inside rein positions the horse and the outside rein limits the shoulder. Also, engage throughout your body, increasing positive tone.

What Is the Horse Learning?

To take more weight on his hindquarters/load his inside hind. Improved canter. Lowering of the haunches and shifting weight onto the haunches. Heightened willing cooperation and collection.

What Is the Rider Learning?

The rider refines her seat aids, her timing for the limiting aids, the feel for definite collection and refinement of the aids.

Heads Up! For Western riders, I would recommend Exercise 7.5 here. You can also ride this exercise with just 4 cones or 3 cones (as a triangle).

What to Do if...?

My horse runs forward.

Your lateral aids or, respectively, your limiting aids are not coming through to your horse. This is also often a sign that the use of the reins was too strong. Calm your horse and then begin again, first by riding half-pass at the canter (see *Exercise 9.4*).

Try counting along very deliberately with your canter strides.

My horse breaks when he gets tired.

Give your horse time to build up his muscles. This is a strenuous exercise. Better to ride the exercise correctly once then take a long walking break on a loose rein.

Tip: In your mind, count along with the canter strides and remember to praise your horse!

10. Special Exercises (Not Only for Western Riders)

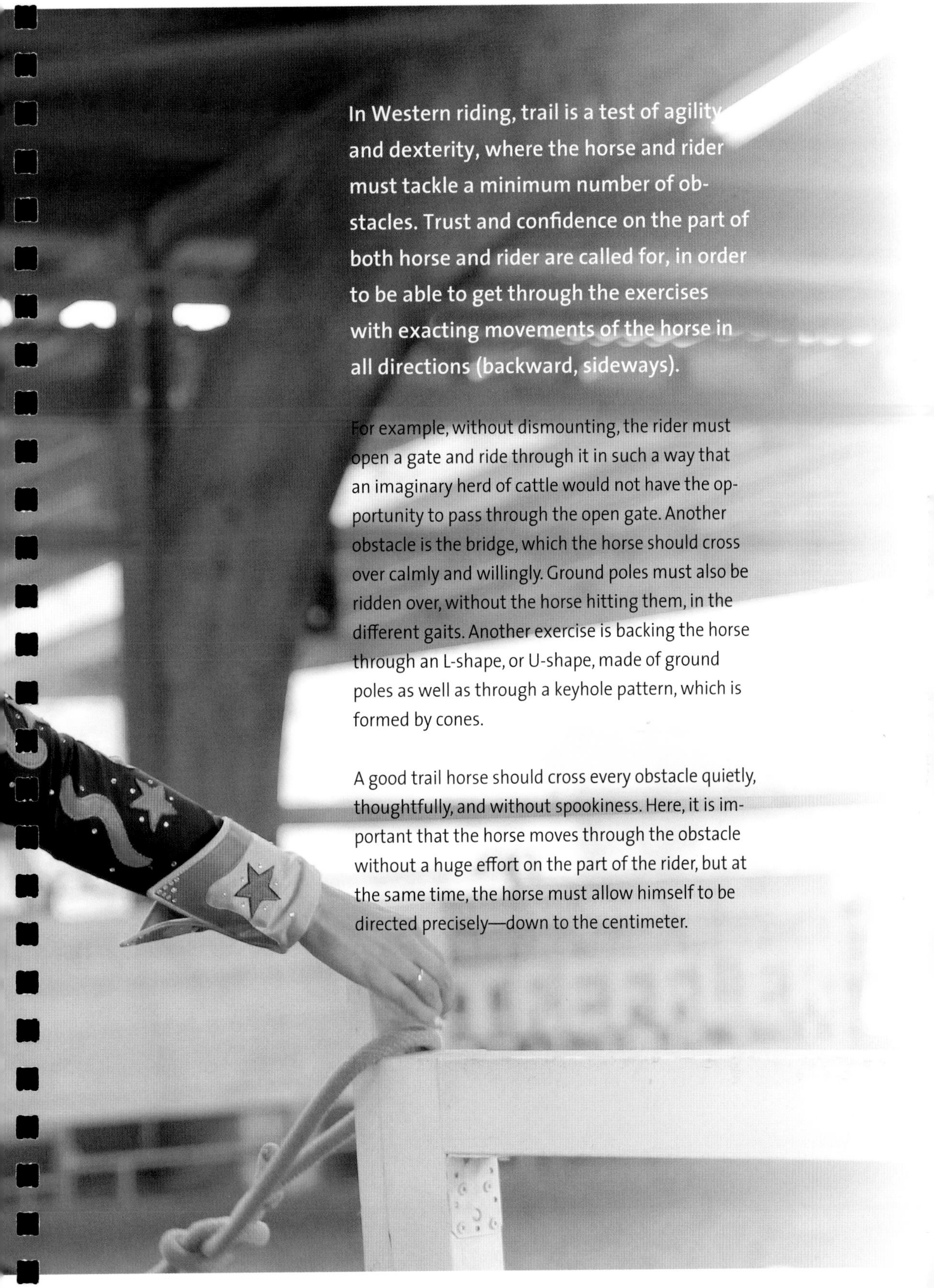

In Western riding, trail is a test of agility and dexterity, where the horse and rider must tackle a minimum number of obstacles. Trust and confidence on the part of both horse and rider are called for, in order to be able to get through the exercises with exacting movements of the horse in all directions (backward, sideways).

For example, without dismounting, the rider must open a gate and ride through it in such a way that an imaginary herd of cattle would not have the opportunity to pass through the open gate. Another obstacle is the bridge, which the horse should cross over calmly and willingly. Ground poles must also be ridden over, without the horse hitting them, in the different gaits. Another exercise is backing the horse through an L-shape, or U-shape, made of ground poles as well as through a keyhole pattern, which is formed by cones.

A good trail horse should cross every obstacle quietly, thoughtfully, and without spookiness. Here, it is important that the horse moves through the obstacle without a huge effort on the part of the rider, but at the same time, the horse must allow himself to be directed precisely—down to the centimeter.

10.1 Box

With this exercise, you can school tight turns. The goal is to ride a small volte inside the square. The horse learns to move diligently forward while making tight turns and to step up with his hindquarters. For Western riders, this exercise is an integral part of trail courses.

What Do I Need? 2–4 ground poles each about 6.5 feet (2 m) long, 1 cone.

Setting Up

Position two ground poles at a right angle to one another. The poles should be touching, so that there is no gap. Position the cone in the middle of the diagonal line formed between the two "open" ends of the ground poles. Add a third ground pole, so that you have an open square. The cone can now be eliminated. Close up the square with the fourth ground pole.

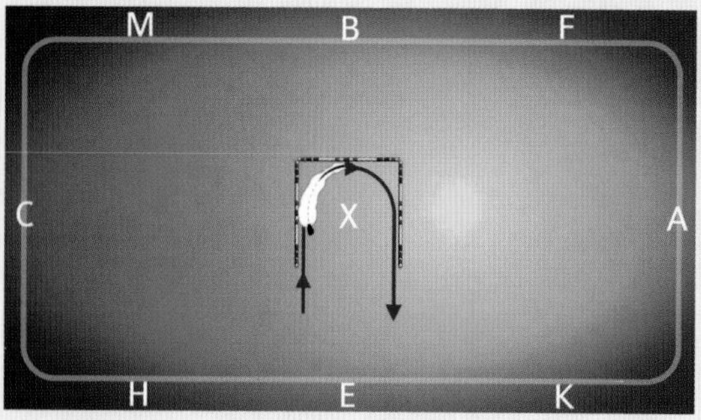

Diagram 1

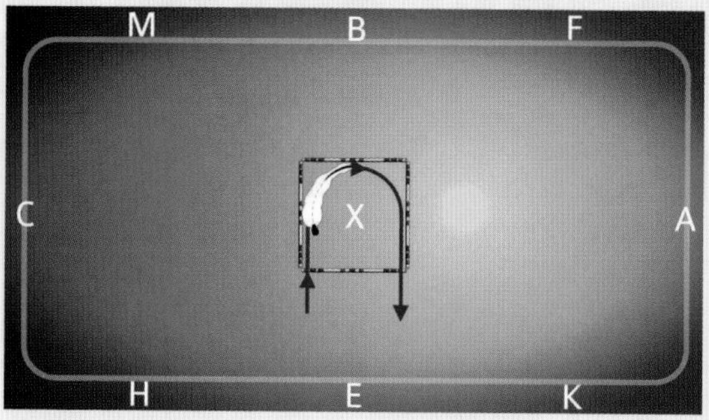

Diagram 2

How Does This Exercise Work?

(1) At the walk, ride into the two-sided corner made of ground poles and try to ride a volte around the cone.
(2) After the volte, ride back out of the two-sided corner.

Heads Up! Don't fold at your hips. Try to lift high through your breastbone.

(3) At the walk, ride into the square on the open side. Begin your turn as soon as the horse's last hind foot crosses the open side. Only begin positioning your horse to the right after you have started your turn. Ride with minimal bend and exit the square at the open side (diagram 1).

Heads Up! Move straight ahead as you enter the open side of the square. Only begin to position your horse when you begin your turn. Ride straight ahead as you exit the square on the open side!

(4) Riding straight ahead, enter the square by riding over a ground pole. Turn and ride straight out over the same ground pole (diagram 2).

Heads Up! Make sure that your horse never loses his forward movement.

(5) Tracking right, ride straight into the square. Turn as in diagram 3. After one volte, exit the square on the opposite side from where you entered (diagram 3). Or, ride one-and-a-half voltes, then exit over the same pole as you entered (diagram 4).

Tip: Follow the turn with your upper body.

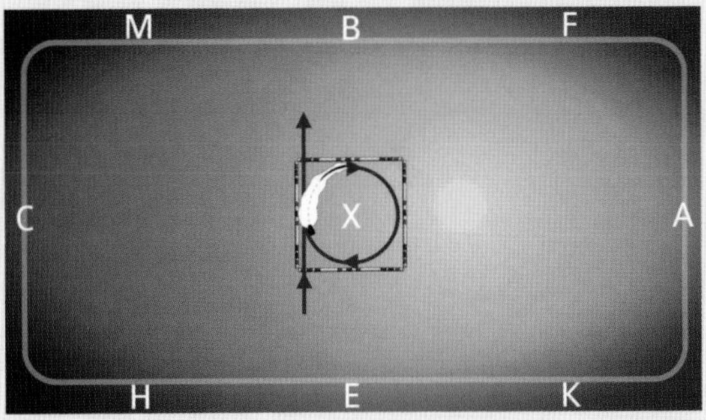

Diagram 3

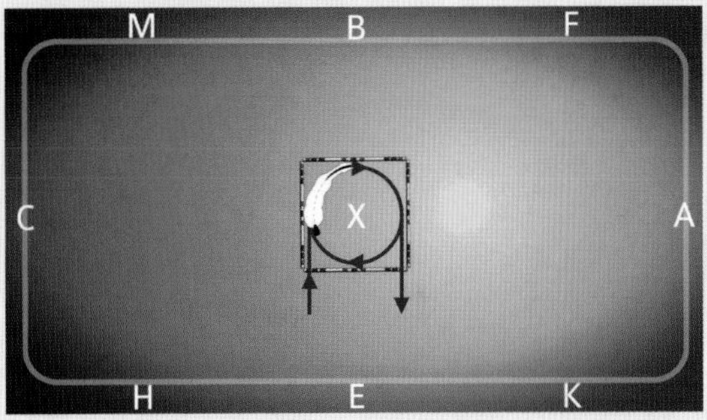

Diagram 4

What Is the Horse Learning?

Coordination. To step up with his hindquarters. How to complete tight turns with correct positioning.

What Is the Rider Learning?

Proactive, forward-thinking riding, and directional planning. To ride tight turns. →

Stay to the right as you cross over the first pole, in order to then turn left within the box.

An opening inside rein helps the horse to complete the tight turn within the box.

What to Do if...?

My horse hits the ground poles.

As you cross over the poles, make sure that your hands are almost lying on the withers. Your reins stay long, so that you don't disturb the horse with them. Lift your breastbone and follow through with your hips, so as to avoid blocking the horse. Drive the horse over the poles with a quiet stride. If he trips anyway, try to practice walking over the poles separately from this exercise. Praise your horse when he does not trip!

If, while crossing, your horse catches his last hind foot on the pole, you should count the steps as he crosses, and first begin your turn only when all four feet are within the square.

My horse gets slow during the turn or even comes to a complete stop.

Drive with your legs. If this doesn't do the trick, go back to Step 1. Begin with a larger volte and then make the turn smaller, bit by bit.

10.2 Backing through an L-Shape

In the trail-course task "L-shape," you are practicing backing up. You promote concentration and willing cooperation in your horse. This exercise is motivating and fun.

What Do I Need?

2 poles about 10 feet (3 m) each, 2 poles about 12 feet (4 m) each.

Setting Up

Position the poles to form an L.

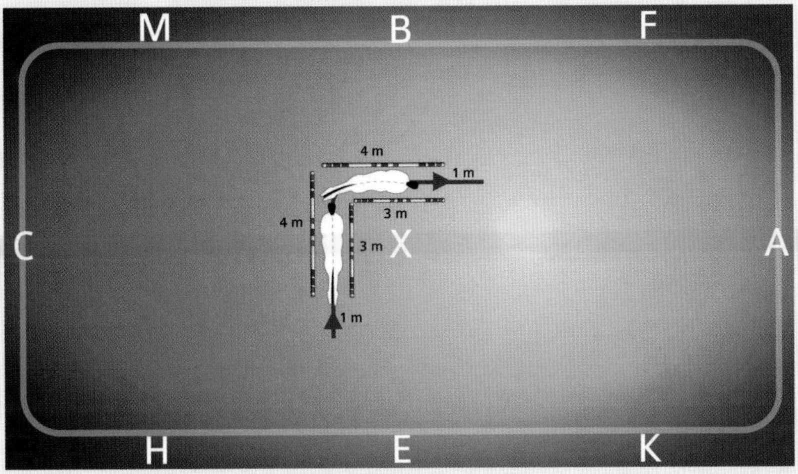

How Does This Exercise Work?

(1) In trail, the L-shape is often ridden backward. Approach the L at the walk, then before the opening, execute a turn-on-the-haunches or turn-on-the-forehand. As soon as the horse's hind legs are in front of the opening, begin backing up. Go backward one step at a time.
(2) Shortly before the corner of the L, position your horse to the outside and allow him to step around the curve. Now, your horse should continue backing in a straight line to the end of the poles, until it can leave the L.

What Is the Horse Learning?

Concentration and obedience. Willing cooperation.

What Is the Rider Learning?

Concentration. Spatial planning. Refinement of the aids.

What to Do if...?

My horse anticipates this exercise.

Practice backing up. With every step, the horse should be willing to wait for your signal. That needs to be happening before you begin this exercise.

10.3 Keyhole

With this exercise, you improve the horse's gaits with diagonal movement. You achieve better balance and more willing cooperation. The keyhole is a component of a trail course. This exercise is ridden backward.

What Do I Need?

3–6 cones.

Setting Up

Position the cones along the centerline at a distance of about 3–6 feet (1–2 m) apart for beginners. More advanced riders can try at 3 feet (1 m) and "experts" can decrease the distance to 1.5 feet (.5 m). Position the cones as shown in the diagram.

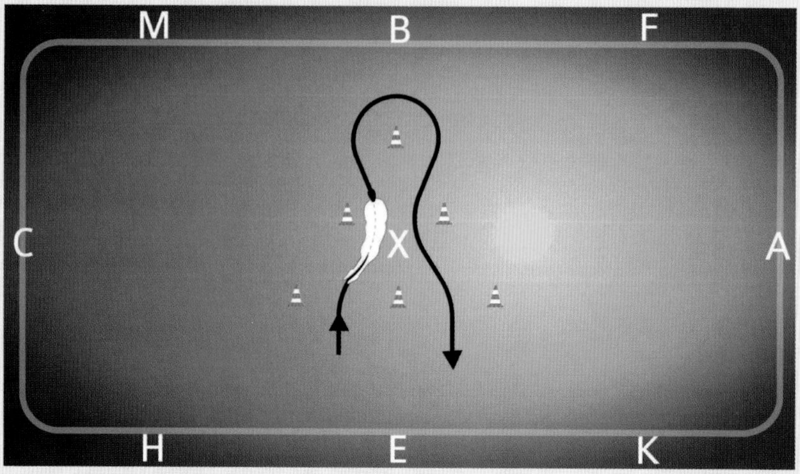

How Does This Exercise Work

Ride backward through the keyhole. The lines that you are riding backward should not touch one another. The horse should learn to respond to the weight aids (also see *Exercises 3.7 and 4.2*).

Aids: If you wish your horse to turn to the right, you must position the horse to the left, weight the left side, and apply your leg aids as you would for backing up.

What Is the Horse Learning?

Trust. To yield to the rider's weight and reins.

What Is the Rider Learning?

Trust. Correct application of the aids. The rider is practicing body awareness.

Heads Up! Take lots of breaks, praise your horse, make sure that motivation is maintained and the horse does not become stressed.

Tip: Only look around the pattern when the horse is standing still—not when he is backing up.

Nena trusts her rider and backs up willingly.

10.4 Side-Pass

In this exercise the horse learns to maintain his balance and coordinate his steps. This exercise enhances motivation and concentration for both horse and rider.

What Do I Need?

1–2 ground poles.

Setting Up

Position the poles 4–6 feet (1.2–1.8 m) from the rail on a long side.

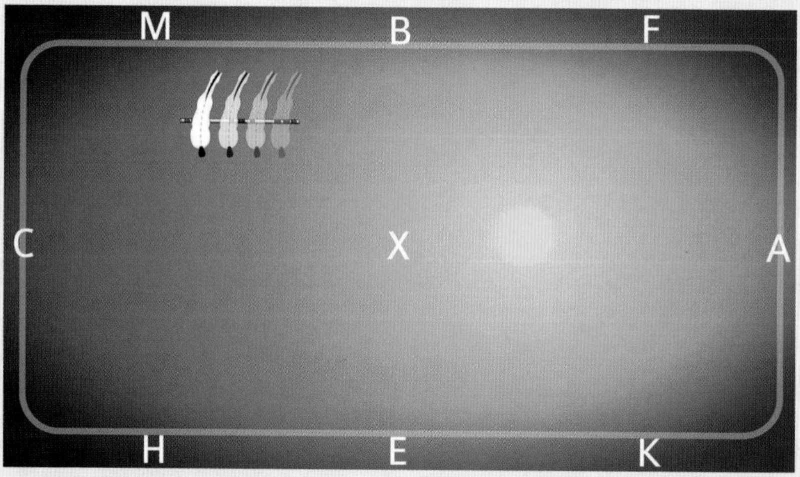

How Does This Exercise Work?

(1) The goal of this exercise is to move sideways over the pole, at a 90-degree angle to the pole. The pole lies under the horse's belly. The horse moves only sideways, in place of any forward movement. Ride a normal leg-yield along the arena rail, with the horse's head facing the rail. Make your horse aware of your aids and be sure—step by step—that the horse is moving sideways along a straight line. Then position your horse in the direction of travel and allow him to assume longitudinal bend.

(2) Next, ride the same way along the pole. The pole lies in front of you and serves as a visual aid.

(3) Ride to the pole at a 90-degree angle. Stop over the pole. Now give the aids for a leg-yield and allow your horse to step sideways until he reaches the other end of the pole.

(4) Position your horse near the pole at a 90-degree angle. Now shift into a side-pass and move sideways to the other end of the pole.

In side-pass, the horse is lightly bent in the direction of travel.

What Is the Horse Learning?

Surefootedness and leg coordination. Agility and balance while moving laterally. Concentration and motivation are enhanced.

What Is the Rider Learning?

Refinement of the aids. Lateral movement. To develop her feel for where the horse is placing his feet.

What to Do if...?

My horse is tripped up by the pole and does not pass over it properly.

Find a second person who can help you guide the horse as he passes over the pole.

10.5 Gate

This exercise is an essential element for trail courses in Western riding. For riders in every discipline, this exercise develops concentration, the "step-by-step" riding through an exercise and attention to the aids. Backing, turn-on-the-forehand, side-pass, or leg-yield are all encompassed within this one exercise. When riding a trail course at competition, you must complete the exercise without coming to a stop.

What Do I Need?

1 gate—alternatively, you can secure a rope on two jump standards.

Setting Up

Position your gate with enough room on all sides, either within your arena or in another area where you ride regularly.

How Does This Exercise Work?

(1) The goal is to ride smoothly through the gate, so that you conclude the exercise with turn-on-the-haunches. Here's how you begin: Approach the gait at the walk. The horse's shoulder should be about even with where the gate is fastened.
(2) Stop the horse and place your hand that is on the side of the gate onto the gate itself. Pause to organize your thoughts.

Heads Up! It's important that this hand remains on the gate throughout the entire exercise. From now on, you're riding one-handed!
Heads Up! Throughout the whole exercise, no part of the horse's body can come into contact with the gate.

(3) Direct your horse backward, two or three steps, until his head is level with where the gate will open. Allow your hand to slide backward along the gate as the horse backs. Pause for a moment.
(4) Now begin to push the gate open with your hand. When the gate is open, direct the horse through. Stop and pause shortly when the horse's croup is level with the gate. The front end of the horse has passed through the gate. Now allow your horse to move his haunches two to three steps around the forehand (as in a turn-on-the-forehand). The hind portion of the horse passes simultaneously through the gate.

(5) Now the rider needs to close the gate. Allow your horse to move sideways toward the gate (side-pass or leg-yield). Close the latch of the gate and ride away from it.

Heads Up! Do this exercise one step at a time. The horse should not get into the habit of barging through the gate. Insert pauses in the right places. As soon as you and your horse have internalized the exercise, you can forego the pauses.

What is my horse learning?

To pay close attention to the rider's aids. The horse is gymnasticized effectively through the various turns.

What Is the Rider Learning?

Proactive riding and refinement of the aids. Concentration and serenity.

> **Tip:** If you want to praise your horse during a pause, you can lower your hand and stroke your horse's neck. When riding a trail course in competition, you may not make it obvious that you're praising your horse. But by lowering your hand (without stroking him) you signal to the horse that he has done everything just right.

What to Do if...?

My horse is afraid of the gate.

Familiarize your horse with the gate first during groundwork. Also, under saddle, proceed slowly and cautiously. Praise your horse for every stride that he takes in the right direction. Always insert pauses. If needed, a helper can support you by opening and closing the gate so that you can just concentrate on your horse.

My horse barges through the gate.

Consider whether this has to do with fear or with lack of respect. If it is lack of respect, insist on the pauses. If your horse steps ahead, back him up instead.

My horse turns too widely, away from the gate, so that I have to let go of the gate.

Check your seat. You must always stay close enough to the gate so that you can open and close it with a lightly extended arm. If you have to lean way out of the saddle, you won't be able to give the correct weight and leg aids. With incorrect seat aids, the horse will drift away from the gate.

The side-pass doesn't work here.

Take time for the side-pass. Make sure that you are not folding at your hips and leaning too far out of your saddle. Otherwise, the horse will take to heart your seat aids, which you are not really intending to give. Use your outside leg and rein to limit your horse on the outside.

10.6 Bridge

With this exercise, you can practice crossing over a bridge, meaning a stretch of track with an unfamiliar surface. At the same time, you are training goal-oriented riding, stride by stride.

What Do I Need?

A bridge or a piece of wood 98 by 35 inches (250 by 90 cm), a ground pole.

Setting Up

Position the bridge along the rail or along a fence line, which provides a boundary for the horse. Place the ground pole 16–24 feet (40–60 cm) away.

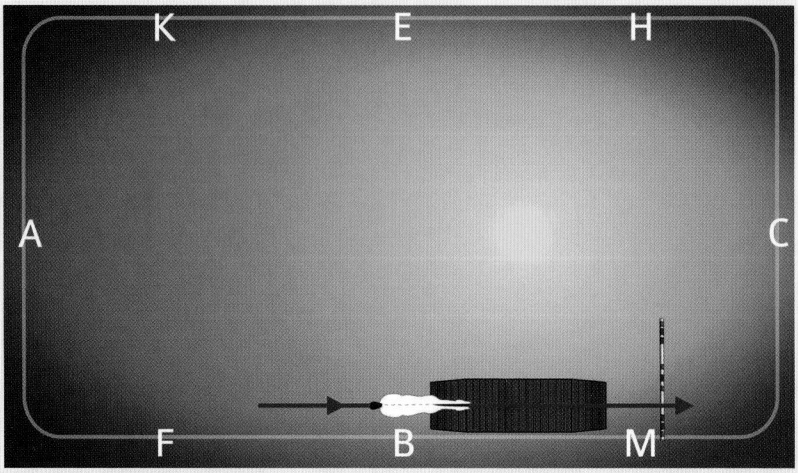

How Does This Exercise Work?

(1) Goal One is for the horse to cross the bridge without hesitation and afterward, Goal Two is for him to step over the pole. First, guide your horse near to the bridge. If he doesn't show any fear, you can ride your horse to the bridge and walk over it.

(2) Praise your horse for every step and build in pauses, so that the horse can process what he has just learned. Only then should you also introduce the ground pole (Goal Two).

What Is the Horse Learning?

To go on diverse surfaces. Composure. Attentiveness and trust.

What Is the Rider Learning?

Concentration and calmness. Precise riding. Trust.

What to Do if...?

My horse is really fearful of the bridge.

Go slowly. Dispel your horse's fears by introducing him to the bridge during groundwork. Allow your horse to look and snuffle extensively. Praise every step. Lead the horse over the bridge and praise him. Train your horse to go over various surfaces: wooden boards or tarps, for example.

In a Western trail competition, multiple points are deducted if the horse hesitates when approaching or crossing over obstacles.

11. Special Exercises (Not Only for Jumpers)

The exercises in this chapter have to do with gymnasticizing your horse with the help of jumping exercises.

Rider and horse learn to estimate distances, assess obstacles, and maintain a suitable and even rhythm. First of all, a good seat and balance are an important foundation. Rider and horse build trust. The rider learns to stay centered when approaching the jump and over the obstacle. For horse and rider, these jumping exercises bring a good variety to jumping training as well as to dressage and pleasure riding. First, these exercises loosen the horse. The activity of his back (bascule) is strengthened and his overall leg technique advanced. Strength and the building of muscles in the forehand, haunches, and back are developed. Jumping trains springiness. Young horses must be introduced to jumping in small steps. Horses who have had bad experiences with jumping can rebuild trust with these activities.

Here are the measurements for distances based on an average canter stride of just under 12 feet (3.6 m)

For one canter stride: 23–26 feet (7.1–8 m)
For two canter strides: 34–36 feet (10.4–11 m)
For three canter strides: 47–49 feet (14.3–15 m)
For four canter strides: 59–61 feet (17.9–18.6 m)
For five canter strides: 70.5–74 feet (21.5–22.5 m)
For six canter strides: 82–97 feet (25–29.5 m)
For seven canter strides: 93.5–97 feet (28.5–29.5 m)

When calculating distances, your horse's stride, the type and construction of the obstacle, footing conditions, and size of the riding area all play a role.

Heads Up! The distances must be correct. Therefore, use a measuring tape when setting up jumps. Be fair in how you build the obstacles, and for safety, consider adding wings. The following applies to all work over fences: please wear a helmet and be sure to have a helper on the ground (a safety vest is a good option, as well). If you have questions about what distances are suitable for your horse, please discuss the exercise with your riding instructor.

11.1 Ground-Pole Pick-Up-Sticks

With this exercise, you school a precise approach and assessment of obstacles. You develop an eye for distances, learn to ride a suitable canter rhythm, and find the correct route on course. Soon-to-be jumping riders can do this exercise at the canter, simulating a show-jumping course.

What Do I Need?
4–6 ground poles.

Setting Up
Randomly distribute the ground poles in the arena or riding area. Don't place them along the path of any arena figures or other known lines. Try to find ground poles of various lengths and colors—this will make the showjumping course more interesting to the horse's eye.

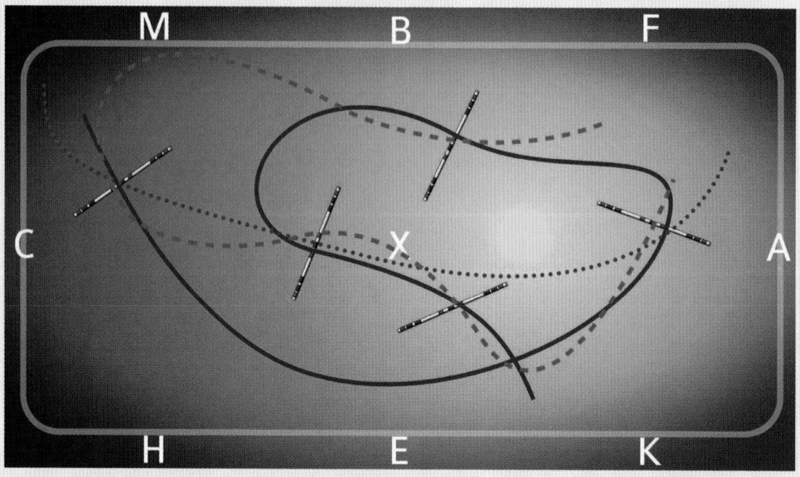

How Does This Exercise Work?
(1) Before you begin your course, think about which path you want to take. Seek out the quickest, the shortest, or the most complicated way with lots of turns.
(2) Choose the gait that is appropriate for your training level and intention. Make sure to maintain an even tempo. Concentrate on each individual pole, riding purposefully to each one. Ride proactively, looking ahead!
(3) Make sure that you are straight as you approach and cross each pole. Take contact evenly on both reins in a timely manner so that you send the horse forward evenly from both legs.

What is the Horse Learning?
Balance, maneuverability, and rhythm.

What Is the Rider Learning?
To maintain an even tempo and ride her horse proactively.

What to Do if...?

My horse always misses a pole.

Reconsider the way you've chosen to go through the course and your tempo.

At the canter, we never arrive correctly at the pole.

Count your canter strides (as in *Exercise 4.5)* and position two to three cones accordingly (at the right distance for your horse's strides) ahead of every pole. Now, ride your chosen path. Lengthen or shorten your strides as you approach the pole so that your horse's strides correspond with the cones.

Praise your horse as soon as he goes over the poles without tripping.

11.2 Ground-Pole Roundabout

This is a calming exercise for hotter horses and good for finding an even canter stride.

What Do I Need?

This exercise can be set up using either cavalletti or simply with ground poles.

Setting Up

Position four ground poles or cavalletti on a circle, at an equal distance from one another. They should be 4–6 feet (1.2–1.8 m) from the rail. There will be a pole at C and X and the others are on the remaining two points of the circle.

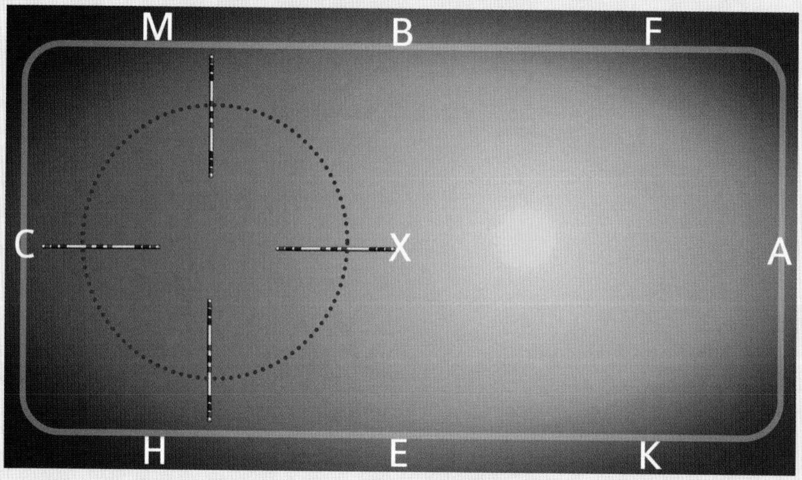

How Does This Exercise Work?

(1) Ride your horse on the circle, over the obstacles. Allow your horse time to find his own rhythm. Only then begin to support your horse with your aids, if needed.
(2) Shorten or lengthen the canter stride in order to improve the rhythm.

Tip: Try to support your horse with your seat and aids and not to interfere with him! Be very elastic through your heel and keep your legs relaxed against the saddle, so that your light seat (for jumping) stays quiet and harmonious.

What Is the Horse Learning?

To find his rhythm, become more secure, and relieve stress.

What Is the Rider Learning?

To maintain an even rhythm on a bending line.

Ground poles encourage even canter strides.

What to Do if...?

My horse jumps into counter-canter or he cross-canters.

First practice this exercise on the longe line without a rider in order to allow the horse to find balance and strengthen his canter.

My horse contracts so much that he hops upward instead of cantering.

First practice with a single ground pole and praise your horse when his strides are even and ground-covering.

11.3 Planning the Course—Counting Strides

With this arena setup, you can plan various courses, count canter strides for various distances, and choose from suitable courses and distances.

What Do I Need? 4 jumps or 4 cavalletti.

Setting Up Position the jumps or cavalletti as indicated in the diagrams.

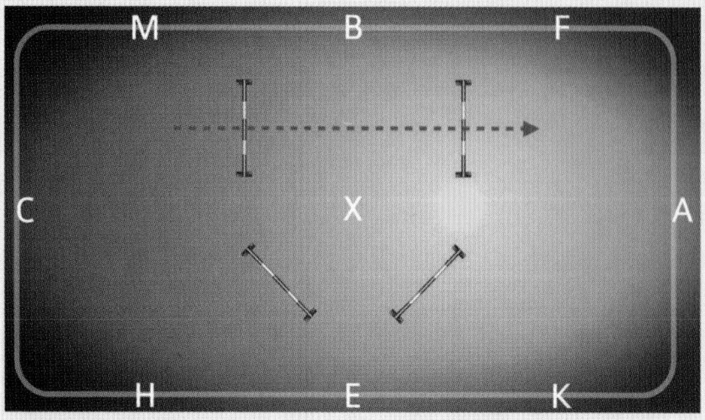

Diagram 1

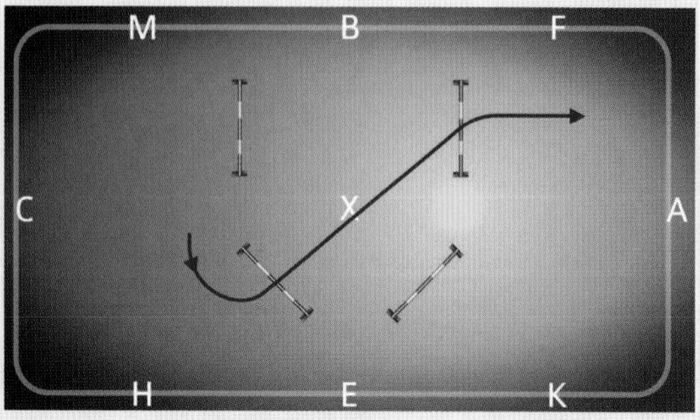

Diagram 2

How Does This Exercise Work?

(1) Start out with three different distances (see p. 142): the distance for the line in diagram 1 is *six* canter strides; the line in diagram 2 is *four* canter strides; the line in diagram 3 is *five* canter strides. Count your canter strides, and shorten or lengthen the strides accordingly. As soon as you can maintain an even tempo as you ride these separate line combinations, refer to diagram 4 and ride the entire course.

What is my horse learning?

To maintain an even tempo at different distances for jumping.

What Is the Rider Learning?

To ride the right tempo for the required distance, to develop her eye for distances, and take the horse back or lengthen his canter stride, respectively.

What to Do if...?

He just feels so out of control.

Choose to start with the line in diagram 2 for this horse, keep the jumps low, and sit back down in the saddle immediately after the landing. Look ahead and ride the horse from the leg and weight to the bridle.

My horse often stops at the jump or runs out.

A horse refuses within a line of jumps for various reasons. If your horse (or you) are nervous about jumping, lower the height of the jumps and proceed conservatively.

Choose a definite, but not overly rushing, base tempo, and praise your horse for every step of progress. Often, horses run out on a line when the distance is not suitable. First double-check the distances and fix them, if necessary. Then, as needed, adjust the distances according to your four-legged friend's size and the length of his canter stride.

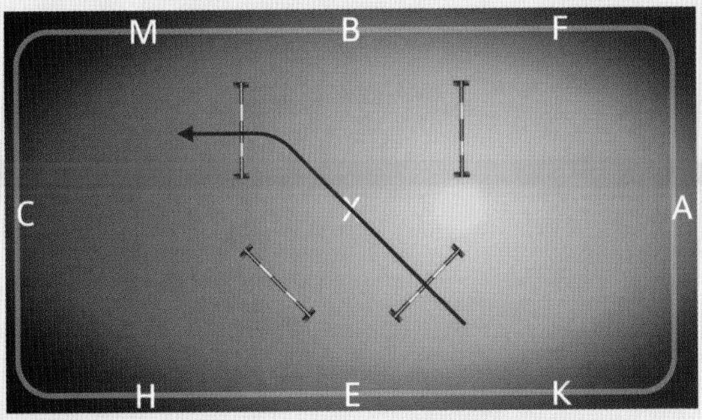

Diagram 3

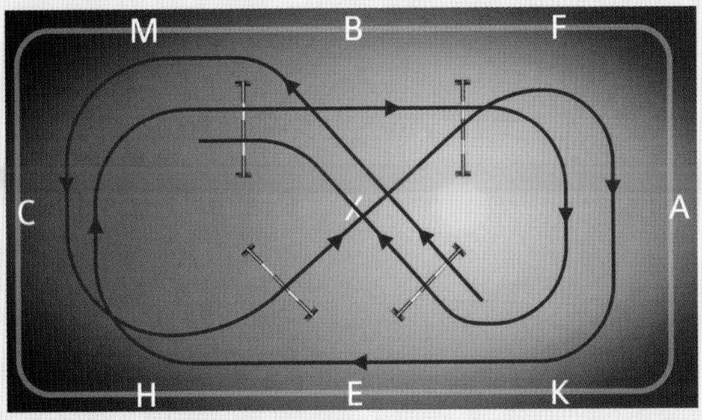

Diagram 4

On straight lines, look ahead through your horse's ears.

11.4 Gymnastic Row

Gymnastic rows are suitable for improving concentration and responsiveness. Coordination between forehand and hindquarters is encouraged and the back muscles are trained. Gymnastic exercises over fences are ideal preparation for jumping and builds trust between horse and rider. In a gymnastic row, the rider is learning to adjust with flexibility to the horse's movement over jumps, improving her feel for rhythm, and developing her eye for distances in between jumps.

What Do I Need?

Jump ends and poles.

How Does This Exercise Work?

(1) Begin with ground poles and cross rails so that you can more easily identify the center of the obstacle. Later, you can up the jumps to verticals. In order to improve rhythm, I recommend you position your fences from small to large. For example: ground pole, 10 feet (3 m); cavalletti cross-rail, 10.5 feet (3.2 m); cross-rail, 11.5 feet (3.5 m); cross-rail, 11.5 feet (3.5 m) [all in-and-outs]; then a canter stride length of 23–24.5 feet (7–7.5 m), a vertical fence.

To gymnasticize your horse's back, I'd advise the following set up: two or three ground poles at the trot set 4 feet (1.2 m) apart; cross-rail with a ground line (canter off); 7 feet (2.2 m), cross-rail; 10–11 feet (3–3.5 m), cavalletti; 19.5–21.5 feet (6–6.5 m), vertical; 20–22 feet (6.2–6.8 m), oxer.

For advanced horses and riders: In order to school attentiveness, you can mix small and large fences, like verticals and oxers, into the row. For this modification, incorporate one to two canter strides in between each jump.

Tip: Ride the center of the line. Cross-rails help with finding the center.

What Is the Horse Learning?

Rhythm and improved concentration and responsiveness. Activity in the horse's back.

What Is the Rider Learning?

The light seat (jumping position). To freely follow the movement of the horse's jump. To improve her feel for rhythm. To develop her eye for distances between fences.

A gymnastic row consisting of cross-rails helps horse and rider jump over the center of the obstacles.

What to Do if...?

My horse gets slower in between the jumps.

Opt for fewer jumps in the row and practice with cross-rails first. Begin with *Exercise 11.2* in order to develop the correct muscles in the horse so that he can handle more jumps in a row.

My horse runs out of the row.

Here, the same reason as above may apply. The horse has not yet developed enough power to handle multiple jumps. Border the row with ground poles or your helper, and make the jumps smaller.

11.5 Follow the Line

At higher levels, jumping requires timing, dexterity, and skill in horse and rider. With various variations of following the obstacles, you can learn while "playing" with it all.

Setting Up

Position various jumps/cavalletti along diverse lines, for example, along a ring figure or a random line in the arena. Incorporate different distances, but carefully follow the measurements guidelines for distances and combinations (see p. 142) and adjust the distances according to your horse's needs.

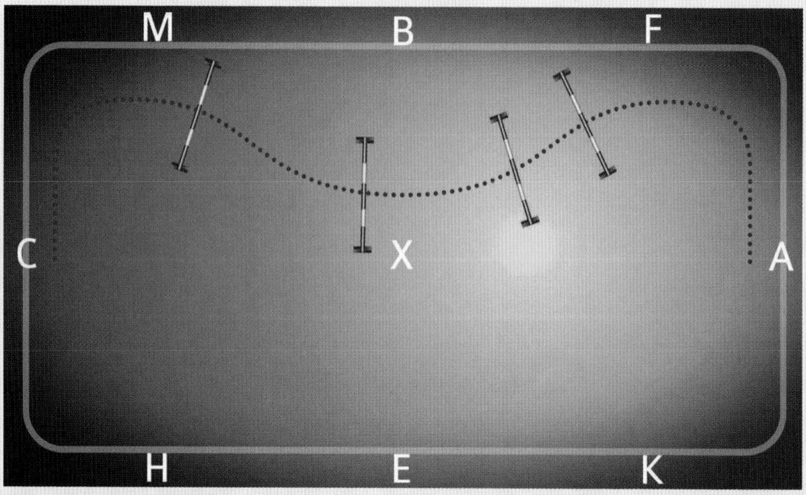

How Does This Exercise Work?

(1) Choose a specific basic tempo for the jumping pattern and hold to this. When you're jumping multiple fences one after the other, it's important for the horse to maintain impulsion and elasticity at the canter. First, begin this training with jumps set at a low height, and seek out the exact point of takeoff. To help, you can even position a cone parallel to show where you want to take off.

(2) Take off from close to the jump. Thus, you'll have a steeper trajectory over the jump, which has a braking effect. A longer takeoff encourages the horse to land closer to the fence, which lengthens the distance he must travel to the next fence.

What is my horse learning?

Increased rideability. Lengthening and shortening of canter strides. Jumping on both curves and straightaways. Balance and equilibrium. To react obediently to the rider's seat and overall influence.

What Is the Rider Learning?

Improved technique over fences, timing, and the feel for takeoff in terms of distances and combinations. Control over tempo and rhythm. Estimating distances.

On bending lines, the rider's gaze tracks to the next jump while in the turn.

What to Do if...

My horse gets slower in between fences.

Finding the right tempo and a suitable rhythm for a distance is elementary. Drive with your legs and try to keep your horse in flow. Additionally, a hesitant or overzealous takeoff can change the tempo and disturb the flow. Decrease the height a bit and reassure your horse. Try not to hinder your horse's movement with added pressure on the reins and go with your horse in a light (jumping) seat. Before attempting the course, carefully think about distances, how may canter strides to incorporate, and stick to your plan. If you find this difficult, you can also position ground lines or cones to help you organize the takeoff.

Thank you...

To everyone who has guided, supported, and motivated me during the creation of this book. The list is long, but then the work on this book was a long process.

First and foremost, I would like to thank all the horses that I have worked with, for challenging me to come up with new training concepts. I deliberately do not use the term "problem horses," as, in fact, in his own way every horse wants to be treated as an individual, and you will not make him your friend by asking him to conform to a preconceived idea. Through the great variety in my daily work, I am over and over again put to the test and must get new ideas for exercises that will effectively support any given combination of horse and rider.

I also want to thank all of my riding students who have come to me with their questions, which I've had to think over.

A special thank you goes to Jessica Huster, my friend of many years, and the author of the first chapter. (Thank you, Jessy, for your constructive criticism, your review of my work, and revision of the first chapter. You are simply the best!) I also want to especially thank Monika Agler, leader of Team-Werk, who came to me with the idea to compile all the exercises in this book, and Team-Werk for providing all the diagrams. Thanks to Meike Jacobson, my editor in Germany, who was very patient with me. To Martin Gaiser, who has constructed the best training situations for us, and supports me daily as a good friend. Thanks to Franziska Weber, Berit Wolf, and Jasmin Ziegler for the wonderful photos that grace this book.

And a huge thank you to Mara Di Girolamo, who supports me every day at the barn, and all the other barn girls who stand by my side every day with advice and action. A special thanks goes to my parents and my boyfriend. Thanks that you are always there for me and support me in every way.

To end I must again thank my four-leggeds, who teach me so much and have made me into the person who I am today.

Ann Katrin Querbach

Index

Page numbers in *italics* indicate illustrations.

Activity of the Hindquarters
exercises for improving, 84, 103, 110, 123 (*see also impulsion entries*)
in Western riding, 3, 88
Aid coordination exercises
Dancing, 27–28, *27*
Shifting the Forehand Over, 20–21, *20–21*
Shifting the Haunches Over, 22–23, *22–23*
Turn-on-the-Forehand, 24–25, *24–25*
Turn-on-the-Haunches, 26–27, *26–27*
Aids
obedience to, 84
overview, 17–19
release of, 51
sequence of application, 18
Three Point Rule of, 19
timing of, 92
visual, cones and poles as, 30
Anticipation, by horse, 29, 65, 66, 91
Artificial aids, 17
Asymmetry. *See also* Straightness
of horse, 23, 75, 100
of rider, 6
Attention span, of horse, 19, 54

Back
of horse, strengthening, 63
of rider, alignment of, 5
Backing up. *See* Rein-back exercises
Bascule, 142
Bend
aiding for, 43, 102, 103
direction of travel and, 100
exercises for improving, 37, 41, 53, 71, 74–75, 109, 116
in neck, false, 76
riding corners for, 116
with straight lines exercise, 107–8, *107*
straightness and, 100
Box obstacle, 130–32, *130–32*
Breaks, importance of, 31
Bridge obstacles, 140–41, *140–41*

Canter pirouettes
basic exercise, 126–27, *126*
preparation for, 110
Canter/lope
counter-canter, 104, *104*, 113, 147
counter-volte at, 117–18
counting strides, 57–58
departure from volte, 53–54
half-pass at, 121–22
in haunches-in, 110–11
impulsion at, 88
lead changes, 112–13, 117–18, 121–22, 125–26
on long rein, 49
shoulder control in, 125–26
stride lengths, for jumping, 142
Cavalletti, 58, 146, 148, 150, 152
Centering exercises
about, 4
Deep Breathing, 13
Finding Your Center, 6, *6*
Relaxed and Following, 12
Sensing and Feeling, 10–11, *10*
Turn Yourself Around, 8–9, *9*
Walking on the Horse, 7, *7*
Change of rein
across the diagonal, 34–36, *34–35*
in Double Square exercise, 70
Changing Tempo, 96–97, *96–97*
Classical Training Scale, 3
Collection, 3, 114
Collection and total willing cooperation exercises
about, 114
Canter Pirouette, 126–27, *126*
Cone Game 2 (with Half-Pass), 123–24, *123*
Counter-Volte at the Canter, 117–18, *117*
Half-Circles, 118–120, *118–19*
Half-Pass at Canter, 121–22, *121–22*
Riding Corners, 116–17, *116*
Shoulder Control, 125–26, *125*
Combining Lateral Movements, 106
Cone Game exercises
basic, 78–79, *78*
with half-pass, 123–24, *123*
Cones, as visual aids, 30
Connection. *See also contact entries*
exercises for improving, 37, 52, 55, 83, 85, 102
hips as point of, 12
in Western riding, 76, 114
Contact
activating the hindquarters and, 88
errors of, 76–77
overview, 76
in Training Scales, 3
Contact and softness exercises
about, 76–77
Cone Game, 78–79, *78*
Crossing the Street, 85–86, *85–87*
The Diamond, 81–82, *81–82*
Leg-Yield from the Rail and Back, 84, *84*
Leg-Yields with Transitions, 83, *83*
Trotting Poles, 80–81, *80*
Counter-canter
basic exercise, 104, *104*

flying changes and, 113
in Ground-Pole Roundabout, 147
Counter-flexion
in controlling shoulders, 20–21, 104–5, 124, 125–26
on the volte, 38–40, *38–39*
Counter-pressure, pressure and, 65
Counter-Volte at the Canter, 117–18, *117*
Counting strides
basic exercise, 57–58, *57*
in course planning, 148–49
Crookedness, 73, 95. *See also* Asymmetry
Crossing the Street, 85–86, *85–87*

Dancing, 27–28, *27*. *See also* Aid coordination exercises
Deep Breathing, 13
The Diamond, 81–82, *81–82*
Direct rein, 18
Distances, in jumping, 142. *See also* Counting strides
Double Squares, 69–71, *69*

Ear-Shoulder-Hip-Heel line, 4
"Ease," 3
Elasticity, 3
Elbow-Hand-Horse's Mouth line, 4, 18
Exercises, generally
benefits of, 2
format overview, 3
Extended trot
from shoulder-in, 92–93, *92–93*
from volte, 94–95, *94*
Eyes, of rider. *See* Gaze, of rider

Figure Eight, 74–75, *74–75*
Finding Your Center, 6, *6*
Flying changes
basic exercise, 112–13, *112–13*
with half-pass, 121–22, *122*
preparation for, 117–18, 125–26
Follow the Line, 152–53, *152–53*
Forehand. *See also* Turn-on-the-forehand
elevation of, 114
falling on, 27, 82
leading with, in lateral movements, 84, 100
Forward energy
as correction for leaning, 76–77
leg aids for, 17
on long rein, 48
straightness and, 69
in transitions, 65
Frame, of horse, 48–49, 76, 77, 83
Front end. *See* Forehand

Gate obstacles, 138–39, *138*
Gaze, of rider, 5, 8, 74, *75*, 85, 119
Green horses. *See* Young horses
Ground poles
Pick-Up-Sticks exercise, 144–45, *144–45*
rider feel for, 10–11
Roundabout exercise, 146–47, *146–47*
spacing of, 58
stumbling over, 80
as visual aid, 30
Guarding leg aids, 17
Gymnastic Row, 150–51, *151*
Gymnastics and mobility exercises
about, 29–30
Backing through Slalom, 45, *45*
Change Rein across the Diagonal, 34–36, *34–35*
Counter-Flexion on the Volte, 38–40, *38–39*
Half-Pirouette with Poles, 32–33, *33*
Shoulder-In and Turn-on-the-Forehand, 43–44, *43*
Simple Serpentine, 37–38, *37*
Spiraling In on a Circle, 41–42, *41*

Half halts, 19
Half-Circles, 118–120, *118–19*
Half-pass
about, 100, 102
at canter, 121–22, *121–22*
in Cone Game 2, 123–24, *123*
for falling in on shoulder, 27
in other exercises, 98, 106, 107–8, 112, 123, 127
transition into, 106
Half-Pirouette with Poles, 32–33, *33*
Halts and halting, 19
Hand position, 5, 18
Harmony, 2
Haunches. *See also* Turn-on-the-haunches
activity of, 84, 88, 103, 110, 123 (*see also impulsion entries*)
engagement of, 38, 83, 114, 116, 126
falling out on, 86, 110, 117
leading with, in lateral movements, 84, 100, 106
Haunches-in
about, 100, 102–3
benefits of, 109
on half-circle, 110–11, *110*
Haunches-out
about, 100, 102–3
benefits of, 109
schooling circle with, 109, *109*
Head position, 76, 77, 83
Hind end. *See* Haunches
Hips, folding at, 49

Impulsion
at canter, 88
loss of, 86, 94, 153
in Training Scales, 3
at trot, 120
Impulsion and activation exercises
about, 88
Changing Tempo, 96–97, *96–97*
Extended Trot from Shoulder-In, 92–93, *92–93*
Extended Trot from Volte, 94–95, *94*
Stop Sign, 98–99, *98–99*
Trotting on from Rein-Back, 90–91, *90–91*
Inside/outside aids, 69, 105

Jumping exercises
about, 142
Follow the Line, 152–53, *152–53*
Ground-Pole Pick-Up-Sticks, 144–45, *144–45*
Ground-Pole Roundabout, 146–47, *146–47*

Gymnastic Row, 150–51, *151*
Planning the Course, 148–49, *148–49*

Keyhole, 134, *134–35*

Lateral movements. *See also specific movements*
benefits of, 100
combining, 106
Lead changes, flying, 112–13, 117–18, 121–22
Learning, by horses, 14
Leg aids
about, 17–18
in correcting line of travel, 69
in turning, 8
Leg position, 5
Leg-yield
in Cone Game, 78–79
from rail and back, 84, *84*
with transitions, 83, *83*
Lengthening, of strides, 55, 58
Lifting the Back, 55–56, *55–56*
Lines, of rider's seat, 4
Long rein, riding on, 48–49, *48*
Lope. *See* Canter/lope

Motivation, of horse, 19, 30

Neck, false bend in, 76

Obedience, to aids, 84
On the Inside Track, 105
Opening rein, 18, 49

Pacing, 44
Planning the Course, 148–49, *148–49*
Plumb line, of rider's seat, 4
Praise, 14, 19
Precise Transitions, 64–66, *64*
Pressure, counter-pressure and, 65

Rail, dependence on, 105
Refusals, in jumping, 148–49
Regulating aids, 17, 18
Rein aids
about, 18
contact and, 5, 76
resistance to, 76–77, 83
riding on a long rein, 48–49
in transitions, 65
Rein-back exercises
basic, 50–52, *50*
Keyhole, 134, *134–35*
other exercises using, 110–11
through L-shape, 133, *133*
through Slalom, 45, *45*
trotting from, 90–91
Reining, exercises for, 94
Relaxation
mental vs. physical, 62
signs of, 63
in Training Scales, 3
Relaxation and suppleness exercises
about, 62–63
Double Squares, 69–71, *69*
Figure Eight, 74–75, *74–75*
Precise Transitions, 64–66, *64*
Serpentines, 67–68, *67–68*
Zigzag Ground Poles, 72–73, *72*
Relaxed and Following, 12
Renvers. *See* Haunches-out
Resistance, avoiding, 3
Rhythm, in Training Scales, 3
Rhythm exercises
about, 46
Canter Departure from Volte, 53–54, *53–54*
Counting Canter Strides, 57–58, *57*
Lifting the Back, 55–56, *55–56*
On a Long Rein, 48–49, *48*
The Rein-Back, 50–52, *50*
Trot-Canter Transitions, 59–60, *59, 61*
Riding Corners, 116–17, *116*
Running out, in jumping, 148–49, 151
Rushing, 86, 93, 139, 148

Safety considerations, for jumping, 142
Schooling the Circle with Haunches-Out, 109, *109*
Seat
exercises for finding, 4–14
importance of, 4–5
weighting of, 6
Self-carriage, 3, 83
Sensing and Feeling, 10–11, *10*
Serpentine exercises
benefits of, 31
Shifting the Forehand Over, 20–21
Simple, 67–68, *67–68*
Shifting the Forehand Over, 20–21, *20–21*
Shoulder, of horse
controlling, 125–26, *125*
falling in on, 27, 99, 117, 124
falling out on, 105, 110
Shoulder position, of rider, 4, 18, 93
Shoulder-in
about, 100–102
from extended trot, 92–93, *92–93*
with turn-on-the-forehand, 43–44, *43*
Side Pass, 135–36, *135–36*
Sideways movement. *See also* Lateral movements
aiding for, 17, 83
in gate obstacle, 139
side pass, 135–36
"Silence is praise enough," 14
Simple Serpentine, 37–38, *37*
Softness, 3, 76. *See also* Contact and softness exercises
Spiraling In on a Circle, 41–42, *41*
Standing still, 91
Stop Sign, 98–99
Straightness
about, 100
in line of travel, 97, 108
in Training Scales, 3
Straightness exercises
about, 100–103
Bending and Straight Lines, 107–8, *107*
Combining Lateral Movements, 106
Counter-Canter, 104, *104*
Flying Changes, 112–13

Haunches-In on the Half-Circle, 110–11, *110*
On the Inside Track, 105
Schooling the Circle with Haunches-Out, 109, *109*
Stretching exercises, for riders, 7
Stretchy frame, 18, 48–49
Stride length, 142, 148–49
Strides, lengthening of, 58
Stumbling, 65, 80
Suppleness, 3, 63. *See also* Relaxation and suppleness exercises

Tempo
changes of, 40, 96–97, *96–97*
in jumping, 152, 153
maintaining/regulating, 49, 94, 95
Tension, 2, 62, 102
Three Point Rule, in aiding, 19, 83
Total Willing Cooperation, 3, 114. *See also collection entries*
Trail exercises
about, 128
Backing through an L-Shape, 133, *133*
Box, 130–32, *130–32*
Bridge, 140–41, *140–41*
Gate, 138–39, *138*
Keyhole, 134, *134–35*
Side Pass, 135–36, *135–36*
Training, horse's learning in, 14
Training scale elements, 3
Transitions
benefits of, 54, 58
in The Diamond, 81–82
from haunches-in to haunches-out, 109
leg-yields with, 83, *83*
precision in, 64–66
rushing, 86
in serpentine exercise, 67
trot-canter exercise for, 59–60
in Trotting from Rein-Back, 90–91
Travers. *See* Haunches-in
Trot
canter-trot transitions, 59–60, *59, 61*
extended, from shoulder-in, 92–93, *92–93*
extended, from volte, 94–95, *94*
with ground poles, 80–81, *80*
half-circles in, 118–120, *118*
impulsion at, 88, 93, 120
from rein-back, 90–91, *90–91*
rhythm of, 46
Trotting Poles, 80–81, *80*
Turn Yourself Around, 8–9, *9*
Turn-on-the-forehand
basic exercise, 24–25, *24–25*
in half-pirouette exercise, 32
with shoulder-in, 43–44, *43*
Turn-on-the-haunches
basic exercise, 26–27, *26–27*
in half-pirouette exercise, 32
in Stop Sign exercise, 98
Turns. *See also* Bend
exercises for improving, 8–9
inside box obstacle, 130–32
quality of, 98

Voice aids, 19, 66
Voltes, 3, 94

Walk
improving quality of, 44
rhythm in, 46
Walking on the Horse, 7, *7*
Warm-up exercises, 30
Weight aids
about, 17
exercises for improving, 8–9
Western riding
aids in, 18, *51*
canter pole spacing, 58
hindquarter activation in, 88, 103
recommended exercises, 94, 98, 118, 124, 126, 128–141
rider position in, 4
Training Scale for, 3, 76, 100, 114

Young horses
aiding for, 18, 19
exercises for, 34, 54, 104, 132

Zigzag Ground Poles, 72–73, *72*